Learning to
Commit

the best time
to work on
your marriage
is when
you're single

Avrum Nadigel

Interna

Self-Counsel Press acknowledges the financial support of the Government of Canada through the Canada Book Fund (CBF) for our publishing activities.

Printed in Canada.

First edition: 2015

Library and Archives Canada Cataloguing in Publication

Nadigel, Avrum, author
    Learning to commit : the best time to work on your marriage is when you're single / Avrum Nadigel. — First edition.

(Reference series)
Issued in print and electronic formats.
ISBN 978-1-77040-245-4 (paperback).—ISBN 978-1-77040-450-2 (epub).—ISBN 978-1-77040-451-9 (kindle)

    1. Marriage. 2. Relationship quality. 3. Marital quality. I. Title.
II. Series: Self-counsel reference series

HQ734.N32 2015   646.7'8   C2015-903691-7
                                                      C2015-903692-5

Self-Counsel Press
(a division of)
International Self-Counsel Press Ltd.

Bellingham, WA   North Vancouver, BC
USA   Canada

Avrum Nadigel's Learning to Commit *offers fresh perspectives for those interested in building an intimate, long-term relationship. It is much more than a self-help book. In a lively and informative narrative, Nadigel combines frank personal experiences, practical considerations, and an accessible account of the theory and practices in the field. Specifically, he bases his practice on systemic theories.*

He poses a series of questions, based on hard earned realism, that will leave the reader in a much better position to acquire the evaluative skills needed to achieve an emotionally satisfying coupledom: "Who am I?", "What do I have to offer?", "What do I need in a partner?", and, most importantly, "How do I become the partner that I am seeking?"

For Nadigel, the key to success lies in the process of individuation, which results in a solid separate sense of Self: not in a merged identity. One is seeking not to be completed, but to share oneself completely with another on an equal basis. For this, it is essential to use all our resources to assess the validity of our choices and decisions. In a series of graduated steps, he leads the reader through the steps that result a clear understanding of what is entailed in finding a compatible partner with whom one can achieve a long term successful, intimate relationship.

— Hanna McDonough, psychotherapist and former lecturer, Department of Psychiatry, University of Toronto

When dating it's so easy to get caught up in fantasies of what life with someone else might be like. But with all those imagined possibilities, how can you stay grounded and focused on creating a relationship that you'll be happy with in real life? This easy-to-read and substantive book urges you and *gives you tools* to figure out what you're about so that you can pick a partner who's right for you for the right reasons."

— Dr. Rachel Ptashny, psychiatrist

In a book world loaded with relationship advice, Avrum Nadigel's Learning to Commit *stands out as a major contribution to understanding how our relationships can be improved. While its focus is on the commitment-phobic person, he provides useful information for all couples who are attempting to navigate their way to a better relationship. His style is clear, understandable, and entertaining. He vulnerably provides examples of his own problems with commitment and how he worked through them. In addition, he gives many other real, clinical examples of difficult relationship issues that most of us can identify with. His wise insights and his knowledge of the principles that make for better relationships are accessible and solid. Nearly every page offers useful information for making it through the challenging world of developing good relationships.*

— Ronald W. Richardson, author of *Family Ties That Bind*

Avrum, this book is such a clear and easily understood manual on how to find and keep a relationship with oneself and with others. It manages to synthesise some of the most profound of concepts into one user friendly guide to conscious living and loving. I cannot wait to teach from it, and to give it as a gift. Your writers 'voice' is wonderful.

— Adrienne Gold, educator and former TV personality

I loved this book! Few self help books have kept my attention from beginning to end. Those that do I recommend to my patients. An enjoyable read chock full of valuable information and insights backed up by important theoretical perspectives. I will definitely recommend this book to anyone, single or coupled, who is struggling with relationships and those who need to reflect on family of origin issues to understand their present and improve their future.

Dr. Laurie Betito, Psychologist, Sex and Relationship Therapist, author of *The Sex Bible for People Over 50*, Radio talk show host

Learning to Commit takes the stereotypical other-focused dating paradigm; "What do I want in a partner? What are the qualities I'm looking for? Who speaks my love languages?" etc, and turns it on its head. Instead, it asks, "What am I bringing to the table?" And, "What am I willing to do to about it?"

Using stories from his own life plus synthesizing concepts from various branches of Family Theory, Avrum has written an accessible and useful book about relationships-how to get them, how to keep them and how to improve them.

As I went through the book again to write this review I saw how many times I'd circled a notable paragraph or put an exclamation point beside something I found original and important pertaining to relationship dynamics.

Avrum listed some excellent resources at the end of the book that I highly recommend to anyone who wants to delve more deeply into the topics he's covered. However, the way he's used what he's learned as a researcher, a recovered commitment-phobe, a boyfriend, son, husband, father, and therapist is educational, entertaining, and optimistic. Learning to Commit is helpful on its own terms.

Lorna Hecht, MFT Individual, Couples and Family Counseling

Contents

Notice to Readers

Laws are constantly changing. Every effort is made to keep this publication as current as possible. However, the author, the publisher, and the vendor of this book make no representations or warranties regarding the outcome or the use to which the information in this book is put and are not assuming any liability for any claims, losses, or damages arising out of the use of this book. The reader should not rely on the author or the publisher of this book for any professional advice. Please be sure that you have the most recent edition.

Dedication

This book is dedicated to:

My father, Steve Nadigel of blessed memory, who, on November 6, 1998, made a promise to be a better father, and spent his remaining years making good on that promise.

My mother, Gail Brown, for showing me that change is possible, and that you don't have to be a slave to your history.

My wife, Dr. Aliza Israel, "because there is so much in this life to wonder at, and we've only just begun." You wrote that. You were right, as usual.

The late Dr. David Freeman, for providing me with a lighthouse; a way to navigate the rocky seas of my relationships.

Acknowledgments

I am thankful to so many for the chance to do this, and for their help:

My children — living proof that "(I've) won it … you can sort of tell these things" — Izzy and Sammy. You provide blessings beyond words. I hope this book will be useful to you one day.

To my brother, Robert Nadigel, who demonstrates, on a daily basis, how to, in Seth Godin's words: "Ship."

To Steve Morton, who convinced me that laughter and walking can cure almost anything.

To Drs. John Christensen and Sandy Hordezky for their time, wisdom, and well-placed nudges towards marriage.

To the late Dr. David Freeman for his wisdom, warmth, and reminders to "keep lots of notes, and write a book."

To Avraham Feigelstock for organizing the talk with David Freeman; proof that it only takes an hour to give birth to a new generation. And to Shmulik Yeshayahu and the rest of the Kollel gang for continuing to share their time and services so others can grow with them as I did.

To Kirk LaPointe, who offered to help "in whatever way possible". Twice you made good on that promise.

To Tracey Bhangu and the rest of the Self Counsel Press crew, it's wonderful to have you in my corner.

To Gabe Meranda & Lorna Hecht-Zablow, Ball & Change could have easily been chicken scratch, thank you for making it so much more.

To Motti Rapoport & Relief Resources, a wonderful organization providing exemplary, culturally sensitive mental health services.

This book couldn't have been conceived without the talent, guidance, and patience of Jennifer Tzivia MacLeod, Lynne Grodzki, Ilan Saragosti, and Cathy Presland.

To the Village Shul and Rabbi Ahron Hoch, Adrienne Gold, and Ellie Bass for providing me with a platform to test many of the ideas that have become this book.

To The House and Rabbi Rafi Lipner for taking a chance on a speaker that you knew little about.

To Catherine Rakow for her patience, wit, and guidance as I stumble my way through Dr. Bowen's ideas.

To my clients for allowing me to become an intimate part of their lives and for placing their faith in my ability to help them improve their relationships.

To everyone who signed up for updates about this project. Well, you didn't receive a ton of those, but I hope this book has met all your expectations.

I am particularly indebted to my wife, Dr. Aliza Israel, who, by her actions, teaches me to stand up for what I believe in, and accomplish my goals. She does all of this with humility and grace. I picked a good one.

Finally, to the late Dr Murray Bowen, the founder of Family Systems theory and therapy: We never met, but your ideas have helped me think differently about my closest relationships and by doing so, cleared the path towards my becoming a better man and the optimistic husband and father I might never have become otherwise.

Introduction

Why read a book about marriage and commitment written by a self-pro-claimed commitment-phobe? Because whatever you happen to be going through when it comes to issues with long-term relationships, you should know right off the bat that this is something I've struggled with, too.

Of course, you may wonder if you should buy a book with "marriage" in the title, or in this case, subtitle, at all. Unfortunately, it would be hopelessly awkward to splash the phrase "long-term committed relationship" on the cover and impossible to capture the nuances of every relationship. Please assume that I'm using the term "marriage" as a catch-all for all of these relationships — including yours.

The ideas in this book helped someone who viewed marriage as a death knell, and that someone was me. That's why I'm so eager to share them; as it turns out, sometimes the things we resist the most are actually the things that are the most precious to us.

No, marriage and commitment did not come easily to me, and maybe it doesn't to you, either. If you're anything like the singles and young couples I work with, you probably have varying degrees of cynicism and anxiety about how you will fare in your own marriage. You might ask yourself, "What's the point?" That question is the impetus behind this book, and one that I will hopefully have helped you answer by the time you've reached the final chapter. It's a question that haunted me throughout my dating life, and reared its head during the first year of my marriage.

To quote marriage and sex therapist David Schnarch, "Marriage is not for the faint of heart." It's not hard to imagine why. The often-quoted 50 percent divorce rate (depending on which study you choose) gives people pause about committing to an institution that produces as many failures as successes. Things don't improve when you consider how poorly so many of the other 50 percent are doing. The end result for many of today's singles is a toxic mix of anxiety and cynicism for anything to do with monogamy. At its most extreme, this fear nourishes promiscuity and commitment-phobia, somewhat glorified by the media and relationship pundits.

There are lots of industries looking to cash in on this behavior, for example, Ashley Madison, a well-known online dating service and infidelity-supporting web community. Many of my young-adult clients wonder if monogamous relationships are social and religious relics from the past. Yet, within a few sessions, cynicism and personal defenses give way to fear, then fear to hope: hope that they might have been wrong to doubt monogamy.

I hope to share with you the things I've learned about improving relationships — our own and others'.

This book will be useful for clergy, family mediators, divorce lawyers, parents, and mental health professionals. But most importantly, I believe this knowledge will be useful to you. It certainly saved me from my own inertia and anxiety, and has helped many of my single clients, including some who are getting married as I write this book.

I will do my best to distill this information and make it applicable to your life.

However, I can't promise you top-ten lists or quick fixes. I won't tell you to be more loving, give more hugs, or improve communication. Instead, what I will offer is to guide you towards a better understanding of yourself and the people you love. The work may sometimes be tough, but my guess is you've come to be suspicious of relationship advice that's too easy and doesn't demand anything of you.

With any relationship dilemma or patterned response you find yourself in, you will constantly need to ask yourself, "What is my contribution to this?"

You'll know you're on the right path when old patterns and reactions start to change. You will get to see what you're made of, and move from living out of reactivity towards a goal-directed life.

One request while you go through this book: Please make sure to bring your independent thinking with you to the material. Try some of the exercises, and wrestle with the ideas, but in the end decide for yourself if this information will benefit you. If not, I encourage you to keep looking until you find something else that will work. I wish you luck and courage on this journey.

Finally, about terminology: I will alternate between the terms "marriage," "long-term relationships," and "committed relationships," but the ideas throughout the book pertain to all of them equally. Also, while most of the examples in this book will be of heterosexual couples, the ideas here are equally relevant to same-sex couples.

1
Beginning to Learn

1. My Story: A Fear of Commitment

"We teach what we most need to learn."

— Richard Bach,
Illusions: The Adventures of a Reluctant Messiah

It has only been a decade since I did battle with my own struggles with intimacy and commitment-phobia. In my mid-thirties, and by the time I met the woman who would become my wife, I had a string of relationships, none of which lasted longer than five weeks.

In my late teens and early twenties, my trysts and brief relationships went hand in hand with my indie-rock lifestyle. However, by my late twenties, my friends — most of whom were settling down — lost interest in hearing about my adventures. In time, I became the punch line of a joke, as told by comedian Chris Rock:

> *"Eventually, every man has to settle down. Cause you don't want to be the old guy in the club. You know what I'm talking about, any club you go into there's always one old guy. He ain't really old, he's just a little too old to be in the club."*

But I didn't settle down then; I just avoided clubs. I also did my best to convince myself that I was doing something about my self-imposed allergy to commitment.

Therapy helped to a degree. However, as the years passed, the sessions started to meander and feel self-indulgent.

I asked my therapist, whom I had already been seeing for two years, how much longer he felt we would need to work together. His answer? "Two to three times a week for another three to four years."

The next day, I terminated therapy.

A much cheaper — and hopefully quicker — option was to check out the self-help and relationship sections of my local bookstore. I pored through pages of relationship advice, mining for any hidden gems that therapy had not provided. Instead, the professionals made one thing clear: People like me were beyond repair, so should be avoided at all costs.

I would end each of these self-therapy sessions feeling weary, hopeless, and painfully alone. Yet I never lost hope. Perhaps it was the years of personal therapy or my own training as a therapist, but I understood the pain was a necessary tool for growth.

It would take several sobering experiences, along with the support of friends, and the passage of time, to help me move beyond a crippling fear of commitment.

I'll discuss these later in this book, but just to look at what these experiences were briefly:

1. My introduction to Bowen family systems theory in a graduate program at McGill University.

2. A defining experience leading a group trip to Israel.

3. Establishing a one-on-one relationship with each of my parents.

4. Overcoming my parents' divorce and moving to Vancouver.

5. Meeting Dr. David Freeman, a family therapist who introduced me to some (at first) mind-blowing ideas.

6. Discovering the book *Passionate Marriage*, by Dr. David Schnarch.

As these disparate experiences were influencing my thinking, I found it interesting that they almost all came back, in some way, to Bowen family systems theory.

There are certain ideas that just ring true, from the minute you first hear them. They touch you deeply, and as you carry them around, you find them helpful in many ways. Naturally, if you find such an idea, you hold on to it, and try to put it into practice. And if it works, hold on to your hat: You just can't help becoming somewhat of an evangelist for these ideas ... you want other people to reap the benefits as well if they're that dramatic.

That's why I wrote this book.

> *A lazy part of us is like a tumbleweed. It doesn't move on its own. It takes sometimes a lot of depression to get tumbleweeds moving. Then they blow across three or four states.*
>
> — Robert Bly, *Bad People*

Like most people, my knowledge of how relationships worked was formed by watching my parents. From what I can remember, they had a normal marriage. What I thought was normal, however, was actually a cool indifference, with the occasional blowout. Since the marriages of my friends and extended family seemed about the same, I never wondered if things could be different.

I recall my maternal grandmother sharing stories about the man she almost married, but let get away. Actually, all the stories of misery and regret that I encountered were similar. The stories would end with some variation of the phrase, "And that's how I ended up with your grandfather." The message seemed to be twofold:

1. "If you don't want to end up like us, don't pick the wrong partner."

2. "How will you know you've found the right one? You'll know when you know."

I'd agonize trying to figure out what might happen — emotionally or sexually — to tell me I was with the right partner. I'd wonder whether thinking "you'll know when you know" would eventually turn into me making the wrong choice. These questions, fuelled by fear, consumed me.

I already knew how much was at stake. My mother, who'd always been one of those people clamoring, "you'll know when you'll know," ultimately left my father. Had she failed to heed her own advice and married him despite not knowing? Or had she known at the time she married him, then stopped, somehow?

Whichever was the case, I continued to live, and date, with this idea in mind. I wasn't alone; many people believe this idea. In time, I came to realize it is a false idea that leads many singles off the right track. But that revelation didn't come right away.

Since I wasn't willing to commit to a relationship until I had a guarantee that I was with The Right One, I remained single.

Whenever I was on a date and felt pangs of anxiety or doubt (which appeared with remarkable consistency by the three- or four-week mark of all my relationships), I would become highly critical. I was looking for the smallest of details to indicate I might be with the wrong person. An irritating laugh or blemish would raise my anxiety, nudging me to move on, to keep searching. The reward was always the same: reduced anxiety and profound relief that I had narrowly missed falling into the wrong relationship.

The sum total of these ideas had me abandoning any date or relationship at the first sign of doubt. Meanwhile, friends, family, and other professionals were adamant that relationships shouldn't be as hard as I made them.

All of this became an albatross around my neck, as my commitment-phobia became deeper and deeper entrenched. But the human mind is powerful, and I used it effectively to rationalize my predicament. I told myself smugly that I had outwitted my friends and family; that they were miserably wasting their lives in dead-end relationships.

As a songwriter, I'd romanticize my attempts to stave off commitment with flowery lyrics about independence and truth. I was a maverick forging my own path, different from my friends who had sleepwalked into long-term relationships out of fear of being alone.

One of the first life-changing experiences that got me off the lone-liness train for good happened while I was volunteering for an organization during a summer trip to Israel. The group was mostly composed of university students, with a few middle-aged volunteers, and one man in his sixties.

Curious, I asked the older man why he chose to volunteer on this program. He seemed glad to share details about his life. He told me that he had never married because he was holding out for The One. He expressed some regret about this and mentioned that he was lonely, particularly when he was in his apartment in the United States, so he spent three-quarters of the year volunteering for various organizations in Israel.

He turned to me and asked if I was in a relationship. I said no, and with a bit of a smirk told him that I too hadn't found the right one. His facial expression immediately lost any sense of levity, and he said: "Keep on running, and you'll end up like me."

I watched his lips move, knowing he was right, thinking, "This will be me. I will be alone, in my 60s, traveling the world to avoid sitting home alone … no wife, no kids." I was terrified. But within a few hours I was back to chasing the next passing thing that caught my attention.

Motivational speeches are rarely enough to change our lives. Fortu-nately, time has a way of exposing even the most ardent self-delusions. Perhaps it was turning 30. Maybe it was my parents' divorce, or that my friends were now spending time at home with their partners playing board games, instead of gallivanting with me. Casual sexual encoun-ters — which had once provided adventure and distraction — became meaningless and depressing. Dating was a chore. Thoughts of being alone and childless started to haunt me. It was a time of profound sad-ness and trepidation about the future.

Soon after the divorce, my parents moved on with their lives. I did not. Months of worrying about and advising my parents resulted in my exhaustion, sleeplessness, and anxiety. They moved on, and it was time for me to do the same.

I took Horace Greeley's advice to "Go west, young man." I sold all my belongings and moved to beautiful Vancouver, British Columbia. I'd dreamed of living there since my early twenties, but as with my inabil-ity to commit to a relationship, fear of the unknown also held me back from moving. It took a spiral of worsening panic attacks; the pain of my inertia outweighed any perceived fears of living in Lotusland. So I quit my job and made my way west.

After settling into my new surroundings, I found myself spending time with a group of perpetually single thirty- and forty-somethings. We were a motley crew with differing accents, careers, and reasons for uprooting our lives and resettling in Vancouver. We connected to each other through our loneliness and yearning to establish committed relationships. Every week I'd show up to another event, mustering the optimism to believe that this would be the week I'd meet my life partner. It did not happen.

What did happen was another one of those life-changing experiences: I heard author and family therapist Dr. David Freeman speak at a singles' event held at the local Jewish Community Centre. Picture the host, a Chassidic rabbi — black hat, shiny coat, long beard — standing up to introduce that week's speaker, Dr. Freeman, a tall, clean-shaven New-Yorker, sporting typical therapist garb.

Freeman's thick Brooklyn accent amidst this left-coast audience added to the oddity of the evening. All in all, the quirkiness helped create space and made me curious about what would soon unfold.

For all I thought I knew about relationships (I was a practicing therapist at the time), Freeman debunked many of my own assumptions, for example, that poor communication is the cause of relationship problems. He introduced novel ideas about romantic love, providing subtle warnings that the very things that cause a young lover's heart to flutter can, down the road, be the catalyst of dissatisfaction and divorce. He encouraged us to focus on our own interests, because the more interesting we are to ourselves, the more we have to bring to the table in our relationships.

At the time, I had no idea why his ideas resonated with me. In fact, they shouldn't have. For at least a few months, I was attending the same weekly singles event, with speakers all addressing issues about dating, marriage, and sex. By the time Freeman spoke, every speaker sounded the same, but not Freeman. Why? At the time, I could not answer this question.

Later on, I would learn that Freeman trained with Dr. Murray Bowen, one of the pioneers of family therapy and founder of family systems theory. This would be one of a plethora of disparate run-ins with family systems theory that would become instrumental in my ability to work through my own fear of commitment. Freeman didn't mention Bowen Family Systems theory once, yet his talk moved me, in the same way that Bowen had jumped off the page for me when I had been a student at McGill.

During the question-and-answer period afterwards, I said I'd just ended a relationship and was finding Harriet Lerner's *The Dance of Intimacy* quite helpful. Before I could ask my question, a woman from the audience suggested I read a book entitled *Passionate Marriage* by Dr. David Schnarch. Freeman piped in and said: "Oh yes, Dr. Schnarch is doing very interesting things." I bought the book the very next morning.

Passionate Marriage moved me, by saying things that were contrary to conventional wisdom and somehow instilled me with hope. And throughout those pages, it was Bowen whom Schnarch credited most.

To me, my seemingly random experiences started to feel less and less random, pointing to the power of family systems and how its ideas stood out from everything else out there, providing a compelling argument for marriage.

1.1 A paradigm shift

All breakthroughs, in every sphere of activity, have involved a 'break with'. There is no breakthrough without a change in paradigm. We need to break with the old ways of thinking. The structure of scientific research shows us that breakthroughs require a break with the old ways of thinking.

— Stephen Covey,
in *Director* magazine (2009)

A paradigm shift, according to Stephen Covey, is an experience that changes your perception of how the world works, and leads to profound life changes. For most people, paradigm shifts occur after a significant event happens in your life or family, i.e., a death, the loss of a job, or the birth of a child. For me, a gradual, largely unconscious process of finding Bowen behind every corner crystallized one day over a book.

The unforgettable moment I realized it was happening, I was in a coffee shop, sipping a mocha and reading Schnarch's *Passionate Marriage*.

For years, I had tried to make peace with my seeming inability to commit. I reasoned that some people are marriage material and some people are not; I clearly was not. Then along came Schnarch to inform me that I had it all backwards. He argued that our struggles with intimacy, rather than being a sign of failure, exist to guide us to a path of profound, mature love. He said everyone, even commitment-phobes, is wired properly for intimate relationships. For the first time in years, I was offered real hope that my difficulties with intimacy were not something to run from but to run towards.

Most inspiring among Schnarch's ideas was his belief that one could work on becoming better at intimacy through practice, much as you can strengthen your muscles by lifting weights.

For Schnarch, the key to practicing hinged on differentiation; the ability to separate your own thinking and feeling from other people's, particularly individuals in your own family. In fact, it is the expectations and pressure from our families — with all of their multigenerational, knee-jerk reactivity — that most threatens our ability to function as separate, thinking beings.

When you have your own ideas, and act on them whether alone or in close proximity to those you care about, Schnarch wrote, you can increase your own level of differentiation and, in doing so, become more capable of being in an intimate relationship.

This counterintuitive idea instantly rang true for me. The beauty of this idea for a perpetually single guy like myself was that, according to Schnarch, I could become more differentiated by working on any intimate relationship, not just a romantic one.

Schnarch borrowed the concept of differentiation from Dr. Murray Bowen. I'd first encountered Bowen in graduate school, where his ideas had stood out against the background of the dozens of therapists and therapeutic modalities to which we were introduced. He wasn't the cool kid on the block, or the trendiest theorist out there, but once I encountered Bowen, everything else faded into the background. From psychoanalysis to Cognitive Behavioral Therapy, only Family Systems spoke to me: telling me all I'd ever wanted to know about my family, including the frightening observation that — without a lot of work — bad dynamics get passed down from generation to generation.

I was charmed by the delightfully outrageous story of the origins of Bowen's theories, when he first planned an emotional, nonviolent confrontation with his family. He wrote a series of letters and made several phone calls to his parents and siblings, disclosing family secrets and telling each person what the others had said about them. Within a short time, everyone in his family was furious with him. But when the dust settled, Bowen noticed that:

- Family members were now able to deal with each other directly, rather than going through third parties or keeping secrets.

- Relationships that had seemed stuck were now more fluid and open.

- He was able to heal a distant and conflicted relationship with his brother.

Intrigued by Bowen's example, and I admit, tickled about the idea of creating a ruckus of my own, I decided to give differentiation a try to help repair my relationship with my father; a relationship which was (to put it mildly) strained.

According to family lore, things had been that way for generations. Following Bowen's pattern, I spoke with my father and told him something my mother had told me: that she was thinking of leaving him. She was livid.

"How can you betray our trust like that? I thought we had a special relationship! How can you be so selfish?"

But I was determined to break the triangle of mother, father, son. To develop one-on-one relationships with both parents, and not be a confidant of either, and that is what I did to deal with it. My hope was to put the (marital) problem back where it belonged. If my parents couldn't deal with each other, why would they think that I — their son — could solve their marital issues? Worse, by agreeing to take my mother's side, I drove a wedge between my father and me

. Ultimately, this would take a toll on my emotional well-being, leading to increased anxiety, insomnia, and a paralyzing fear of commitment. And though it took a few years (and my parents' divorce) for change to take place, ultimately, I managed to break this generational pattern and develop a close relationship with my father.

This did not happen overnight, but over the next few years, I was able to establish relationships with both of my parents. By removing myself out of their marital gridlock, they chose to face each other. Ultimately they divorced, found new partners, and moved on with their lives.

Now I was free to choose what type of relationships I wanted with my parents. As you'll discover throughout this book, this was the first — at times grueling — crucial step to tackling my own fears about intimacy.

1.2 Everything coming together

That had happened years before my move to Vancouver and my encounters with Bowen through these new messengers, Freeman and Schnarch. But something clicked now: I realized that my significantly improved relationships with my family were all the evidence I needed to throw my weight behind Bowen. This decision would provide new, but exciting, meaning for the popular lyric from the Sinatra song *New York, New York*: "If I can make it there, I'll make it anywhere, it's up to you ... "

It was up to me, but where to start?

Before I started reading Schnarch, I assumed I couldn't change (yes, even therapists get hung up on bad assumptions sometimes). We assume our roles in our families of origin, and most of us figure they won't change. Delving into Bowen's family systems theory made me realize that not only could I change things, but that if I didn't, I'd probably pass these bad dynamics onto my own children.

A word about family systems theory. Our families are a complex system, made up of relationships, each with their own history, rituals, and functioning. A problem with one person, or one part of the system, impacts the entire system. So, for example, if one of your parents loses a job, it is likely that this will impact you either emotionally and/or in the form of a lifestyle change. Because individuals and systems (families, couples, corporations, etc.), resist change, we do our best to maintain homeostasis. This means that we try to keep things stable or the same. So, to continue the example above, if your mother loses her job, and decides that the family may have to go through a temporary challenging time while she goes back to school, it is predictable that certain members of your family (perhaps the spouse) will push her to get another job — to bring things back the way they used to be.

For our purposes, this basic but compelling observation about how human beings behave, suggests we should do our best to expand our thinking about relationship problems — that there is rarely a smoking-gun, rarely only one person at fault, whether you or your partner. As you'll see in some examples later on, however, this type of process is rarely simple. In my case, it involved establishing one-on-one relationships with each member of my family, breaking existing triangles, and more.

I did the work, and managed to establish a relationship with my father (as previous generations in my family hadn't been able to do with their fathers). Later on, the payoff would be huge.

Even as I worked on all those family issues, I never thought that any of that would help me overcome my issues with promiscuity and commitment-phobia. I still thought they were two separate things. It was only after bumping into family system's ideas over and over through those numerous coincidences (Freeman, Schnarch), that the work I'd done with my father came rushing back to me.

I realized that if this stuff could work with my dad, who knew how it could improve my relationships with women? Although I was still wondering how these lessons in differentiation would apply to my future relationships and help me find The One, I was encouraged enough by my success with my father to start applying these lessons to other family relationships: first my brother, then my mother, although that's not to say it happened overnight.

I knew from reading that attempts to untangle oneself from family secrets and establish one-on-one relationships with family members don't always go smoothly. My family members reacted with anxiety and resistance to change.

They said I was selfish, and when things didn't revert back to business as usual — in the previous story, this took the form of pressure to continue to be my mother's confidant in matters about my father — they would threaten to stop talking to me.

In the past, I would have fought and threatened them right back. I would have taken their reactions personally, and blamed other family members for my misfortunes, perpetuating the negative cycle.

This time around, using the new ideas I'd discovered, I could anticipate and plan for these reactions. This gave me more choice about how I wanted to act with my mother, father, etc.; I no longer had to rely on my primitive "fight or flight" reflex. And with more options, comes less anxiety and stress.

The reason I've started by sharing my story is not because I'm anything special; in fact, for the opposite reason: I think I'm pretty typical. For now, I'm mainly using my own example to show you that:

- I know Bowen's family systems theory works.

- Working on current relationships pays off in all future relationships (intimate and otherwise).

- Improving relationships in your family of origin helps, even when it looks like the current problem has nothing to do with them: in my case, the problem was promiscuity and fear of commitment.

As you'll see, these ideas can help you expand your repertoire of thinking and being with family, lovers, friends, and colleagues. With that, you may find yourself with more options for handling yourself in difficult situations. Whereas in the past, you may have had only two options: run away, or capitulate. Now, you can tap into your own creativity, intuition, values, and principles and take action from the best in you. Don't worry if you have no idea what that looks like. We'll discuss what "the best in you" looks like, and how to cultivate this over time. A nice side benefit is that, when we're able to do this over and over again, we increase our psychological resilience, and with that, we become less reactive, experience fewer psychological symptoms of stress and, ultimately, more loving and satisfying relationships.

Upon my realizations, I wasn't out of the woods yet, but I slowly began to reap the benefits of this work in my dating life. I started dating with an internal, rather than external, focus. I still had criteria for the characteristics I wanted my partner to have, but now I could balance those desires with the big picture of my life's goals, as well as my values and principles.

Incredibly, within a year, I had met my future wife. At the same time, I started seeing the benefits of the work I had done in my own family within my clinical practice.

For many years, I had understood emotional pain as something that is happening inside a person, be it biochemical or psychological. Because of this framework, I'd worked mainly with individuals separate from their partners and other family members.

Now that I'd seen these changes in my own life, and experienced my own radical paradigm shift, I realized I could expand the scope of therapy by involving partners and other family members in therapy sessions. Opening sessions up like this helped me get a richer history of how negative situations had developed, and what forces had led to the current anxiety, divorce, job loss, or depression.

To my surprise, this way of working produced results in weeks, rather than years of individual therapy. Remember how my own therapist had told me we'd need to meet two or three times a week for another three or four years? He was working from the paradigm of psychoanalysis, but I was able to accomplish results much sooner with the tools in this book.

2. How Family Systems Theory Works

I've mentioned how Bowen family systems theory kept popping up "randomly" in my experiences. In reality, it wasn't random; as I said, certain ideas just resonate ... and then, if they really work for you, you want to turn around and share them with others.

In my practice over the years, I've seen the results of Bowen family systems theory. There are a lot of theories out there in psychology, but in this case, I've seen it work over and over again, in my own life and the lives of my clients.

I'd like to briefly explain the core ideas of Bowen theory, to help give you an educated layperson's appreciation of this rich body of psychological, sociological, and anthropological knowledge going back more than half a century (though the core ideas have been around for millennia).

When I first introduce these ideas, clients' feedback is often heartbreaking. Nobody has ever given them tools like these to manage their own relationships. They say things like: "Why have I never heard this before?" "How come my priest or rabbi never mentioned this to me during our premarital classes?" And sadly, "These ideas might have prevented my divorce, or at least would have let me end things way better."

There are some great books about family systems theory out there, including some to help married couples. But why wait for marriage? Most people find that, once they're married, with a mortgage, kids, and deeply entrenched resentments, doing this work is much more difficult. Also, while you're single, you have the ability to see yourself more clearly without the confusion and clutter of a relationship. That's why I wanted to try to share these ideas with singles, and with couples in the early part of their relationship. But it's not just about intimate relationships. More than just your ability to be part of a couple, the ultimate payoff of family systems theory is in healing your ability to be part of all relationships, including those within your family of origin.

The message is a hopeful one: Your struggles are not meaningless, and you can build a long-term relationship that is far better than the ones you've seen so far. So why not start as early as possible?

If you're wondering what any of that has to do with picking the right partner or resolving a current relationship dilemma, here's one of the main tenets of family systems theory: You will only succeed in future relationships in ways you have already succeeded with your parents, siblings, and/or extended families.

Let's say you have trouble being in the same room with your father when he is sad. You find yourself cracking odd jokes; anything to try and cheer him up, and in turn, avoid your own inner discomfort and worry. Over time, you may find that you will bring this reactivity into all of your relationships whenever you're dealing with someone else's sadness, perhaps even your own. You'll most likely end up repeating the pattern in your intimate relationships, and in parenting. Maybe you can see now why it's worthwhile to start improving these family of origin relationships first. Most people are shocked to discover how deeply their current problems are rooted in previous generations.

That's why working on your current relationships, regardless of whether you're single, dating, or married, is so important. Family systems theory is all about improving past and current relationships in order to succeed in future ones.

The payoffs are immense. For me, this work allowed me to turn a distant and stormy relationship with my father into a warm, caring, and honest friendship. I don't think it's a coincidence that soon after our relationship improved, I was less prone to run away from difficult relationships and scenarios. This learning was easily transferable to intimate relationships, so when the going got tough, I was better able to remain calm, not lose myself in escapist fantasies, and ponder my choices. Again, when you increase your options, all difficult encounters become a little less difficult.

Then — no big surprise — this newfound outlook made its way into my dating life. I was better prepared to meet the right woman; I was less anxious about commitment, better able to deal with conflict, and I felt curious, not fearful, about what it might be like to stay with one person for longer than a month. At last, I was capable of committing to the woman I would eventually marry.

That's why I'm excited to share these ideas with you. Many are not my own; I stand on the shoulders of giants in my field. Don't think of me as an expert; I'm just a fellow explorer. Just when I think I've figured any of this out, family reminds me of how much I still have to learn.

I hope I can do the real experts' work justice, and that their ideas will resonate in a way that makes you excited by the possibility of positive change.

2
Rethinking Love

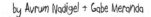

1. Challenge Your Assumptions about Love

"What's love got to do, got to do with it? Who needs a heart when a heart can be broken?"

— Tina Turner, What's Love Got To Do With It

How do you know that your understanding of relationships is correct? Is it possible that some of your ideas, perhaps the most critical ones, are flawed?

Most people trust their intuition about dating, rather than follow a well-thought-out approach. Given the precariousness of so many modern relationships, it would be wise to spend some time thinking about how we have come to our beliefs about love, sex, and marriage.

When I ask my three year old: "What is love?" he answers: "Love is love." A fine answer for a preschooler, but what about for a thirty-year-old? Consider the following questions:

- What criteria should you use when choosing a partner for a long-term relationship?

- What information or feelings would indicate you're in the wrong relationship, or that you should leave the relationship?

- If you were to stop 20 people in a shopping mall and share your definition of love with them, how many would agree with you?

- Is humor an important trait in a relationship? If so, what do you do if you're not funny?

- Where do you turn for guidance and wisdom in the area of love and relationships? Parents? Friends? Hollywood movies? Google searches? God?

- How much physical attraction is enough when deciding if you should agree to a second date?

- Do opposites attract? If so, is there a threshold of difference that you should be cautious about? How different is too different?

- Can you identify where, or who, your answers came from? If you can recall who, say a good friend, or your mother, you might try asking that person how they came to their understanding of these issues.

As a family therapist, I've observed that many of my clients' fundamental ideas about relationships and love were not consciously chosen. They were either faithfully accepted from their parents, or conversely, formed as a reaction to what they saw growing up; they'd chosen to go in the exact opposite direction.

Both of these routes show a feeling-oriented, knee-jerk approach to making decisions about partner selection, marriage, and when to leave a relationship.

If I saw these clients happily succeeding in their relationships, I wouldn't have a problem with a feeling-oriented approach to dating and marriage. Unfortunately, what I see all too often is anxiety, trepidation, and cynicism. To be fair, feelings are a natural way we experience the world and make decisions. But because they're so fickle, they're unreliable as the sole basis for making major life decisions.

For close to two decades, I have witnessed couples decide to leave their marriages and families based almost solely on feelings. They often say things like: "We fell in love, but then somehow fell out of love," or "I love him, but I'm not in love with him."

No wonder so many young people say they're not ready or not interested in committing to a relationship, given how prevalent this transient approach — love coming and going almost at random — has become. However, when young people tell me they are not interested in marriage, my hunch is that their aversion has less to do with establishing long-term relationships *per se*, and more with the fact that they've given so little thought to how they'll handle the natural ebb and flow of committed relationships, and the challenges they bring. How many of your ideas about dating and marriage are truly yours, and how many have been inherited from family, friends, and popular culture?

Whatever you conclude, ask yourself whether you're satisfied with these ideas. Do they make you feel optimistic about your future? Do they give you a hopeful, loving, yet practical roadmap to handling emotionally-committed relationships? Or do they leave you feeling anxious and pessimistic about the odds of successfully partnering?

Instead of inherited ideas that don't work, Hollywood fantasies, or piecemeal advice from Google, start gathering tools and ideas that will help you establish or re-establish relationships on solid, immovable ground.

1.1 What is love?

In the mid '80s, Tina Turner recorded "What's Love Got To Do With It," infuriating romantic poets and relationship-seeking adolescents alike. You need to be careful when you start poking around with sacred ideas such as society's preconceptions about love.

Still, I think the song raises important questions: What is love exactly? Is it something we feel but is hard to define? Perhaps it's an act of commitment, such as standing by someone through sickness and health, 'til death do you part? When one partner asks the other, "Do you love me?" and the other responds, "Yes," does it make any difference if the two people have wildly different ideas about what love means?

Growing up, I was sure I knew the answers. Montreal, the heart of French Canada, is an Old World city dripping with nostalgia and romance. Walk around Old Montreal for five minutes and you will feel how the French language, the ancient cobblestone roads, and some unmistakable "je ne sais quoi" combine to produce an air of romance.

Maybe that's why I felt so painfully alone when I was single on Valentine's Day in Montreal: the short days, long nights, and frigid weather; the city wrapped in the language of love; everyone primed and pumped for a little "amour." I'd avoid cute cafés and restaurants, reminders of the things I did not currently have — love, companionship, warmth — heck, I couldn't even speak French! Outwardly, I scoffed at the notion of Valentine's Day, but inside I desperately yearned for the intense feelings of losing myself in another's gaze, consumed by their sight, smell, touch; oblivious to my daily worries. In short, February 15th couldn't come soon enough.

Not that I was a complete failure at dating. However, those relationships were definitely of the infatuated kind, full of fantasies about how that special person would remake my life for the better. *I'll be happier … and my parents will be thrilled*, I would think.

While I was dating someone, these wishes did, to a certain degree, come true. My weekends, once dreary and bleak, would be full of adventures. Even my songwriting, usually dark and morbid, would take on a giddy tone. Even doing the most boring jobs, I was full of energy, knowing that with each mundane task brought me one step closer to "happiness." But as with most highs, rock bottom was right around the corner, and when it hit, I was left exhausted and confused. Each short-lived relationship nourished my cynicism about the viability of love and commitment.

> *"Love is used as a reason to stay together, and lack of love as a reason to terminate a relationship. This line of thinking is indulged in most often by people who are living their lives based more on emotions than on thinking or inner guidance by principle."*
>
> — Roberta M. Gilbert, *Extraordinary Relationships: A New Way of Thinking About Human Interactions.*

Many of my clients share the feeling-oriented way of experiencing love that I grew up with. They're sure that declaring their love is a first principle, a sign of security and exclusivity. Think how much emphasis we place on the "L" word: who says it first, when, and under what circumstances. We read volumes into whether it's said quickly, in passing; automatically; or with authenticity and depth.

"If my partner can't say, 'I love you,'",they ask me, "doesn't that mean he or she is either emotionally wounded or unsure about me?"

Defining love, or knowing if it means the same thing to both partners, seems less important than making the declaration. I'm sure you can imagine the problems this can cause. Maybe you've even lived through some of them yourself. Perhaps most serious is that love, when we understand it as a feeling, is subject to the same laws that govern all feelings: it comes and goes. And yet, somehow, we expect this feeling, unlike all others, to be permanent.

People honestly believe that how they felt at the beginning of the relationship should be a measuring stick for how well it's going down the road. "If my feelings change, doesn't that mean something's wrong with the relationship?"

I often ask my clients, "Where did you learn that if feelings change, for worse or better, that it has anything to do with the viability of your relationship? "

They're usually stunned. Answers range from general confusion to incredulity: "Everyone knows that if you fall out of love the relationship is over."

Given the poor state of marriage and long-term relationships in our culture, "everyone" is probably the last person you'd want to seek advice from.

1.2 Move beyond feelings: *Jerry McGuire*

> "*The good therapist fights darkness and seeks illumination, while romantic love is sustained by mystery and crumbles upon inspection. I hate to be love's executioner.*"
>
> — Dr. Irvin D. Yalom, *Love's Executioner*

I'm not here to eradicate feelings, or hang poets and romantics in the town square. Emotions are an integral component of human experience, helping us to understand ourselves and our surroundings. When thinking is hijacked by feelings, however, our decisions are erratic, changing as quickly as our feelings shift. If you happen to be a feeling-driven person, falling in love may be especially intense for you, particularly during love-at-first-sight encounters. Unfortunately, this feeling-driven disposition makes you equally susceptible to intense disappointment and disillusionment when feelings inevitably wane. If you're governed by your feeling states, once the feeling ebbs you'll always be left thinking there's something wrong with the relationship (or you).

That's why we all need to develop alternative ways of dealing with intimacy and love. Leveling the playing field, shifting from a feeling-centric position to a balance of thinking and feeling, will give you clarity about what you're looking for and let you make the best use of online dating sites and in-person opportunities when you do meet somebody.

As a therapist, I always find it fascinating to "lift the hood" and peer into the engine that drives romantic love and infatuation. Early psychologists and psychotherapists, starting with Freud, viewed human beings as driven by unconscious energy, an internal force that comprises feelings, habits, thoughts, and automatic reactions. Later, others suggested that this unconscious force was largely responsible for pulling us towards certain people. We choose these people hoping they'll heal unconscious emotional wounds within ourselves. Freeman writes in *Multigenerational Family Therapy*:

"Most people enter relationships with high expectations. Many hope their partners will make up for the losses they experienced in their own families-of-origin. Some carry the romantic notion that finding a loved one will make everything right in the world. These hopes and dreams are brought into a marriage."

You don't have to be a Freudian to see how this plays out in our relationships. Look at how popular movies and books fix the characters' dilemmas by applying the misguided maxim, "love conquers all."

If you want a great example, in my opinion, no movie better depicts the fantasy that love will make up for a person's losses than the romantic comedy *Jerry Maguire* and its famous line, "You complete me."

In the movie, Jerry, played by Tom Cruise, is a late-thirties hard-working sports agent with a past. He's successful, but not happy. His life goes downhill after he's fired from his job, resulting in the loss of all the things he's worked hard for: fame, money, and women. Alone, vulnerable, and teetering on the edge of poverty, he decides to open his own agency, and hires Dorothy Boyd, played by Renée Zellweger. Dorothy, a single mother, harbors a deep yearning to find a father figure for her ill son.

At a time when both are wounded and vulnerable, Jerry and Dorothy are drawn towards each other. Jerry's powerful feelings for Dorothy's son take him by surprise, while simultaneously bringing to the fore Dorothy's desire for a surrogate father for her son.

Each sees in the other a fix for some of their deepest wounds and the answer to profound wishes, past and present. Cameron Crowe, the movie's screenwriter, doesn't offer much detail about the families that Jerry and Dorothy came from. However, there are a number of scenes that allude to Jerry's promiscuity and commitment issues. It doesn't take a degree in psychology to imagine Jerry's childhood wounds and his parents' difficult marriage, which might have lead him towards gratuitous sex and commitment-phobia. Perhaps he hoped that Dorothy's innocence and naïveté would soothe his restless heart, while offering a different type of relationship than the one his parents had. The clues to our current relationship struggles are often found in the way our parents handled their own marriage.

In one of the most memorable romantic scenes of the past few decades, Jerry attempts to convince Dorothy that he's in this relationship for keeps: "I love you. You complete me."

In theaters around the world, every viewer without a heart of stone took part in the collective sighs, tears, and clapping as Dorothy responds: "Shut up. Just shut up. You had me at hello." We cheer for Jerry and Dorothy because we also want to be completed, to feel safe, sexy, and loved unconditionally. And we think we're entitled to feel this way in our relationships.

But notice that we never find out what happens to Jerry and Dorothy past the honeymoon phase. Will there come a time when Dorothy will tire of "completing" Jerry? Will Jerry grow immune to Dorothy's overtures and feel the itch to seek out someone new to regain that feeling? If I were asked to write the sequel to *Jerry McGuire*, we'd probably see Jerry and Dorothy go through what I've seen so many couples going through in my practice: the fallout when they reach the expiry date to "you complete me." My guess is that my dreary sequel wouldn't be nearly as compelling or commercially successful as the original movie.

Unfortunately for many of us, we're so intoxicated with the idea of being completed that when the natural process of waning excitement hits, we feel lost and disillusioned. The profound anxiety about losing this feeling leads to the clichés of failed relationships, like, "I'm with the wrong person," or, "You're not the same person I once knew."

Freeman cautions that if we misunderstand the inevitable loss of early-stages love we will find ourselves always searching for someone new to reignite the "you complete me" process. In the best-case scenario we become serial daters or serial monogamists, jumping from one relationship to the next once we get restless. The worst-case scenario is ending up like CNN's Larry King, married for the eighth time and counting.

So what is it exactly that the *Jerry McGuire* characters, and so many of us in real life, seek to have completed by another person? Let's take a look at a few possibilities through some fictional scenarios. This first scenario deals with the healing of past wounds.

> John's mother died suddenly when he was eight. His father had to work two jobs to support John and his two brothers. The only maternal love was from John's aging grandmother who died when he was a teenager. John describes his upbringing as cold, but safe.
>
> Mary grew up as an only child of an alcoholic mother. When Mary's classmates were starting to socialize and date, she was busy taking care of her mother.
>
> When John and Mary met, it was love at first sight. John was completely taken by Mary's beauty, sweetness, and caring nature. Mary filled his lifelong void for maternal love. Mary felt instantly that John was her soulmate, captivated by his melancholy and his great potential. Like John, Mary didn't realize that being with John let her feel like a rescuer, this time without the harsh realities of caring for someone struggling with alcoholism.
>
> Both fell in love with how the other made them feel: warm and secure. Unconsciously, however, they were drawn to each other by the promise of healing those deep wounds from childhood.
>
> Clearly, "you complete me," however romantic it may sound, isn't always a healthy process that allows the individuals in the relationship to grow and change. This kind of artificial dependency does not bode well for the lifelong stability and health of a relationship.

1.3 Using relationships for validation

> *"There's nothing wrong with wanting to feel validated, accepted and dearly loved. But if you depend on a reflected sense of self, you crash when these aren't forthcoming ... "*
>
> — Dr. David Schnarch, *Passionate Marriage*

Beyond healing childhood wounds, when we're in the throes of newfound love, we expect our partners to make us feel good about ourselves. Dr. David Schnarch understands this dynamic as one person "borrowing functioning" from another. He calls this process a reflected sense of self.

He points out that many people lack a solid sense of self. They only feel attractive when their partner, or some other audience, tells them they're attractive. They only believe they've got a great sense of humor when their partner laughs at their jokes. They only feel creative and productive when their partner provides them with applause or laughs. In the beginning of a relationship, when everything is new and exciting, these things are easy to come by. You might hear a man in a new relationship typically saying something such as, "I love being around Joanne, she makes me feel so special. She always says the perfect things."

If this kind of validation could be sustained forever, relationships would be easy and life would be grand (and I'd be out of a job!). But problems don't wait long to start showing up when one partner relies on a reflected sense of self and the other partner is unable or refuses to constantly affirm this.

Relationships mature over time, and this lessening of affirmation is a natural part of the maturation process for all couples. People are simply unable to sustain the interdependence and infatuation of early love. But when validation wanes, partners feel rejected, hurt, and disappointed. They depended so thoroughly on their partner's affirmation for their self-esteem and identity that they feel empty, even lost. They are disappointed and resentful of their partners' unwillingness to keep on making them feel special forever. And they feel discouraged that they've chosen such an "unsuitable" partner.

As a child, Jordan had a knack for making people laugh. His parents were concerned that their son's interest in entertaining people was actually increasing as he entered adolescence. "How can you make a living in comedy?" they questioned. Whenever possible, they would try to steer Jordan's interests away from comedy towards his education. As a young adult, he started to repress parts of himself that made his parents anxious, turning his back on comedy and acting and focusing on a more traditional career.

Jordan met Michelle at a bar during karaoke night. Slightly drunk, he captivated Michelle's attention with his Michael Jackson impression. She approached like a giddy teenage fan. Jordan lapped up her praise and adoration, and within a short time they were dating.

Early on, Michelle laughed at all of Jordan's jokes and encouraged him to pursue his artistic interests. Jordan would tell all his friends: "Honestly guys, Michelle saved my life. I have never experienced such overpowering love for a woman." He was her "cool half" — it was almost like being married to a celebrity, when a crowd gathered around him.

However, when Michelle became pregnant with their first child, her needs shifted. While his gregarious, fun-loving nature had appealed to her at first, perhaps because she lacked that type of personality herself and reveled in its novelty and exoticism, she suddenly needed Jordan to be a stable family man and worried incessantly about his comedic aspirations.

Now, when he clowned around at parties, she wouldn't laugh; she might even be critical of what she called his immaturity. Jordan started questioning both himself and their relationship. Without Michelle's accolades, Jordan lost faith in his own artistic ability. This reopened deep wounds and caused Jordan a lot of anxiety and angst. For Jordan, Michelle's distance felt the same as his parents' criticism had, all those years ago.

At first, he tried to reason with Michelle: "You know my parents neglected my interests. You always said we'd never let that happen again." However, hard as she tried to please him, pregnancy and motherhood usually overrode her good intentions. When the situation eventually turned nasty, Jordan would remind Michelle of her parents' divorce: "If you really want a different marriage from your parents', you can't abandon me in this way. If this continues, you're going to end up a single parent." Michelle was petrified of losing Jordan, particularly because she swore to herself that she was going to do things differently from her parents. She pushed herself to support Jordan, but this only increased her resentment towards her marriage and herself.

Years later, at a wedding, Jordan was the MC, telling jokes to an auditorium full of family and friends. Michelle found herself seething and disgusted with his narcissism and neediness. She thought to herself, *This is so odd. I used to love this side to him, now I find it revolting. How did we end up like this?*

By now I'm sure you've guessed the answer: she and Jordan relied too much on a reflected sense of each other and not enough on knowing each other on a deeper level, warts and all. As well, they depended on each other for their identity to make up for what they couldn't create on their own.

2. A New Paradigm: Knowing Ourselves

> "I don't expect you to agree with me; you weren't put on the face of the earth to validate and reinforce me. But I want you to love me — and you can't really do that if you don't know me."
>
> — Dr. David Schnarch, *Passionate Marriage*

If Tina Turner is still asking, "What's love got to do with it?" you might see by now why my answer is, "when it comes to romantic love, not really as much as everybody seems to think."

That's because, as we've seen, the intoxicating experience of being "completed" by someone else always has an expiry date. If you choose to ignore this, you'll probably find yourself in another unpleasant but familiar scenario: leaving a relationship to chase down new partners to "complete" you. Or you might end up cajoling and bullying your partner into keeping things the same, ensuring that no one grows in the process. Even if you don't leave, you'll both wind up feeling alone and disconnected, while still technically in a relationship.

But there's a better way of thinking about relationships that can lead to happiness. To get there, we need to take a step back and consider a different, perhaps more courageous way of handling ourselves. As Schnarch states, mature love requires allowing people to know us. To do that, we have to know ourselves. As the saying goes, this is easier said than done.

2.1 How close is too close?

> *"Humanity needs human closeness but is allergic to too much of it."*
>
> — Dr. Murray Bowen

I don't need an alarm clock to wake up anymore. Every morning around 7:00 a.m., my three-year-old wakes up, and does a zombie-like shuffle towards my bed. He stands next to me and says, "Daddy, I want to snuggle." His tolerance for snuggling, however, lasts anywhere from 10 to 60 seconds, at which time he decides he wants to go play with his toys. This is far too short for my liking. I could just as easily fall right back asleep next to him and cuddle for hours. But whenever I try to push for more closeness, my son struggles to get away. Alas, in the name of good parenting, I have to let him go.

According to Dr. Murray Bowen, togetherness and individuality are two opposing life forces that we are all born with. We spend the rest of our lives trying to reconcile their often contradictory impulses. My toddler and I are engaged in the delicate push and pull of negotiating this process, and how I respond to his expressing both of them almost simultaneously will play a crucial role in shaping his future relationships. Of course, I also have a more selfish motive. By giving him the space to decompress by playing with his toys he is able to re-engage with me on his own terms, wandering back to me whenever he feels like it. In a sense, I'm investing in future snuggles, without resorting to guilt trips.

Some lucky people learn to navigate these two forces without too much of a hassle. However, the rest of us grew up in families where there was too much of one and not enough of the other. So, for example, in some families togetherness is all-important, while attempts to separate, even temporarily, are discouraged with guilt and other aggressive tactics. It's not uncommon to hear family members assume responsibility for the happiness and well-being of others.

To point out this extreme closeness to my clients, I'll often joke, "You and your mother are so close that if I pinch her, you scream 'Ow.'"

At the opposite extreme, some families cling to a sense of autonomy at any cost. On the outside, this might even look like maturity and healthy individualism. But beneath the veneer of autonomy, individuals in these families can be highly anxious, with a lot of complicated emotional reactions taking place under the surface.

In these families, people manage their anxiety by not getting too close to anyone. Whenever a significant event — a funeral, wedding, or holiday — threatens to introduce some closeness, individuals in these families can react in one of a number of ways, including exhibiting physical symptoms and emotional distress (such as insomnia, anxiety and depression).

What's the take-away here? Neither extreme is a sign of health. Too much closeness, or distance, in one's family is a response to anxiety. If our goal is healthier relationships, we need to be able to increase our tolerance for both autonomy and closeness.

Some people aren't sure which one they personally struggle with. Either they feel like they're fine the way they are or they don't see the unhealthy side of those family connections.

If you're in this group, try observing your feelings the next time you get together with your family. You'll probably discover you're much more at ease with one — autonomy or closeness — than with the other.

We all carry these emotional dispositions into all of our adult relationships. How much togetherness or autonomy feels right to us drives many of our decisions, from who we pick as our partners to how personally involved we get when discussing hot-button topics. To fully understand how a person can get better at juggling these opposing poles, we need to go back briefly to the theory of differentiation I mentioned earlier.

2.2 Differentiation: Finding a healthy distance

> *"Differentiation is the ability to maintain a non-anxious presence in the face of another's anxiety. It does not mean being uninvolved or indifferent. It is the ability to tolerate pain for growth."*
>
> — Dr. David Schnarch

Bowen's theory of differentiation explains how well a person can function independently by making self-directed choices, while staying emotionally connected to significant relationships. Looking at this in the context of the "individuality paradox," a well-differentiated person has the tools to negotiate the balance between togetherness and individuality.

Those who are lucky enough to be born into a family with high differentiation grow up among people who are firm in their convictions and do not compromise their values and principles due to outside pressure. If pushed to conform or toe the company line, they'd be able to express their beliefs and convictions, and have a clear understanding of what they would and would not do. Also, they could convey their thinking and ideas without bullying, cajoling, or playing the victim. If you disagreed with their ideas, they wouldn't change their thinking just to defuse the tension.

Not surprisingly, much of one's ability to remain differentiated is a result of parenting. When parents are solid in their values and principles, they don't need their child to think like them. Hence the child can develop his or her own opinions without creating too much of a ruckus.

> Michael's mother and father, both die-hard Democrats, still sometimes differed in the causes they supported. While this led to heated discussions, they could both convey their thinking about an issue without needing their partner to support their position. Because they didn't need the other's support, they could occasionally offer it without feeling like they were caving into pressure. When Michael came home from university, he disclosed to his parents that he was a Republican, and would be voting for a candidate that he feared might throw one of his parents into cardiac arrest. His parents were not thrilled, and didn't hide their disappointment. Despite this, they were able to inquire and discuss calmly with Michael the factors that had led to his decision. Because of his parents' non-pressure approach, Michael was able to share his thoughts without fear of hurting his parents.

"If you're paralyzed with fear it's a good sign. It shows you what you have to do."

— Steven Pressfield, *The War of Art*

How many of us have the luxury of having a well-differentiated family like Michael's? Unfortunately, I didn't. As a result, and as I've already shown, my struggle for emotional maturity took place mainly in adulthood (and is still going on). By far the best arena for that to take place has been my marriage. But it began well before Aliza and I actually tied the knot.

As soon as I settled into my identity as boyfriend, my then-girlfriend brought up the topic of marriage. "Marriage!?! I'm not ready for marriage," I responded. To which she replied, "OK, when do you think you'll be ready?" Well, let me think about this for a second … never. What I actually said was, "Well, I want to get married, and yes, to you, but, but, but … "

There were a lot of buts.

I could feel the tide of change lapping at my feet once again, and old reactivity and fear returned. As I had before, I turned to escapist fantasies: Maybe I'm with the wrong woman. I need to find someone as commitment-phobic as I am, who doesn't want to get married.

However, this time around, my catastrophic thinking felt less threatening. More importantly, I did not run from my commitment. It was no mystery that I was finally growing a backbone and the resiliency to stay with my anxiety rather than fleeing. As I'd learned, this is what working on differentiation can do for you.

So we became engaged and for a short time, I enjoyed my new-found status of fianceé. At the hockey rink, changing into my equipment, I enjoyed the attention and catcalls of my teammates for taking the plunge. At work, colleagues seemed genuinely surprised that I was able to take this next step. However, as soon as the first act was over, and wedding planning began, I panicked. My fear led to me to clues that something was wrong. I'd share them with Aliza, but she learned to ignore such things. In the past, her non-reactivity was soothing. Now, it served as yet another reminder that our wedding was around the corner.

Something deep within me needed to create enough chaos to persuade her that all was not right in our relationship. One night I said: "Aliza, I'm not sure I can do this."

She told me to leave, get some sleep, and we'd continue the conversation tomorrow. The next morning, bleary-eyed from sleeplessness, I came back to her apartment and said: "Do you think getting married should be his hard? Are we supposed to be this sad?"

Aliza looked at me and said: "What do you want to do? Do you want to call this off?"

I said I didn't know. She took off her engagement ring, opened my hand, and softly placed it in my palm. She calmly said:"I love you, and I've learned so much over the past few years. But I will not marry someone who does not want to marry me."

By calmly asserting what she would not put up with, she left me to ponder my next move. I thought, I could end this right now and start over. I sat in silence, took my time, and imagined what it would be like to be carefree and single again. But that immature part of myself that had wanted to create relationship chaos? This wasn't what it had expected at all. This was new, grown-up terrain, and suddenly, I realized that after all that work on myself and my family relationships, I, too, was ready.

I chose to stay.

She, of course, was already a grown-up. Her ability to stick to her principles without getting too affected by my anxiety was differentiation in action. She wouldn't play by my rules; indeed, she was playing a game that was entirely new to me. And her refusal to play on my immature terms, to fight and let me dodge commitment, freed me to go deep within myself and really discover what it was that I wanted.

Suddenly, I realized this wasn't about Aliza's desire to get married or her sadness about not getting married, but my own internal desire and value to be in a committed relationship and raise a family together.

What's love got to do with it? Only a little, in the grand scheme of things.

It's easy to write this years later, but at the time, the process was difficult, even grueling. Relationship struggles force us to take a hard look at ourselves, and make important changes that we'd really rather avoid. In my case, I slowly learned to walk towards the relationships, situations, and activities that up until that point I had avoided at all costs.

Sure, this was new terrain; I would need a roadmap to guide my way and techniques to remain calm in uncharted territory. But I also needed to celebrate my successes, to have these small victories to draw upon the next time my anxiety was spiking. (There would be many of these, and there will be many more.)

Can you see how this way of thinking may be of benefit to you? To your relationships? It takes a willingness to grow, and the courage and insight to focus on your efforts, not others. To become a little more curious, calmer, and thoughtful in your relationships. Your attempts to increase your level of differentiation may be easier than my journey has been — or harder. But if you really try to develop a new way of thinking and acting, I believe you'll enjoy the same kind of payoff.

Every decision you make, whether towards growth or towards inertia, has consequences.

2.3 Why compromise fails

> *"Compromise makes a good umbrella, but a poor roof."*
>
> — James Russell Lowell

What's the single most important component of a healthy relationship? Without fail, when I ask a room full of people, they almost all say: "Compromise."

That's when I ask them, "Since most people seem to know this, why do people have such a hard time with their relationships?"

Often, one or more audience members will guess: "Because they are not compromising enough."

Of course, compromise is touted by many so-called relationship experts, so I can see why this is such a universally accepted idea. But once again, I think Julia Cameron's observation is worth repeating: Nothing dies harder than a bad idea. And in the area of emotionally-committed relationships, constant compromising is a pretty bad idea.

As we've seen in previous chapters, when we project our unconscious dreams onto our partner, we feel hopeful, safe, and sexy. Early on in a relationship, these feelings can be very powerful and, if we play our cards right, they really can help us develop strong, healthy relationships. But too often in the early phases of relationships, we try to tip the scales in our favor by hiding parts of ourselves, looking only for commonalities, and doing our best to avoid disagreements.

Since we've spent some time now discussing differentiation, you can probably now see how this would be particularly true for people with low levels of differentiation. For instance, if you are unclear about your own values and principles, you will be keen to agree with most ideas and plans that your partner suggests. Counterintuitively, the opposite is also true: Knee-jerk defensiveness and stubbornness are often a symptom of immature thinking and a sign of poor differentiation.

For many couples, the role of compromise is especially strong when it comes to areas in life that cause either partner the greatest anxiety.

For example, John might sense that sexual innovation causes Stephanie a lot of discomfort or embarrassment. Early in the relationship, he compromises by sticking to familiar positions and not experimenting, even though he would really like to. Later on, however, he might find himself miserable that he's compromised in such an area, and even become angry at Stephanie for denying his physical needs.

When keeping the peace at any cost becomes an essential virtue of the relationship, compromises are exchanged back and forth to ensure that everything remains calm. Couples keep disagreements and differences at bay, and often ignore the proverbial elephants in the room.

As relationships progress naturally, each partner gets used to expecting the same level of compromise and sacrifice of self as they did at the beginning of the relationship. But this level of compromise is virtually impossible to sustain long-term. First of all, what was once novel and exciting becomes rigid and boring. This makes sense when you consider that, by their nature, dating and courtship swirl with novelty and excitement. Early on, even the most mundane conversation — "So, what do you eat for breakfast?" — can result in giggles, smooching, and anticipation of what the future may look like together.

Over time, as the excitement inevitably wanes, so does the couple's motivation to compromise. Accommodation is hard, and we get tired of putting our own wants and needs aside. This is especially true if the compromises include touchy topics like finances, religion, or sex. We may also become increasingly impatient with our partner's anxiety, expecting him or her, at some point, to just get over it.

Many couples come see me after a partner has gotten sick of compromising and tried to assert his or her wants and needs more actively. The partner, naturally, is taken aback, hurt, and angry that the other is changing the rules, and will actively resist any change.

Once the security blanket of compromise is removed, the partners' emerging emotions and anxiety cause great discomfort for both. The result for both is usually deep-seated resentment, an unhappy marriage, and confusion as to why things couldn't have stayed as wonderful as they were in the beginning.

Conversely, couples who go along to get along, continuing to restrict themselves in the spirit of compromise, and avoiding discussion of the issues that might make them anxious or uncomfortable, are left in a "neither here nor there" limbo of dissatisfaction. With a very small sample of acceptable outlets, as the novelty of dating and courtship decreases, both partners are left bored and disconnected, and deeper problems that were masked by the spirit of compromise start to show themselves.

Used to repress one or both partners, compromise is far from the panacea it is widely believed to be.

> On their first date, Julie told Scott she was not a big traveler. Scott loved traveling, but didn't push the issue because Julie seemed like a great catch. A few dates later, Scott told her that he preferred the company of his friends and colleagues to his family. Julie was concerned about this; she was hoping to someday marry and build a warm, close family. However, she figured it was too soon to raise these issues, and complimented Scott on his ability to find relationships that were important to him. As their relationship matured, they learned to avoid the issues that made the other anxious. Scott gave up his desire to travel: He rationalized his decision by thinking that Julie would, over time, change her mind. In turn, Julie avoided bringing up any issues about family, hoping, perhaps, that Scott would change his mind once he was a family man. For a while, these compromises kept anxiety at bay and arguments to a minimum. But over time, both parties started to feel stifled. When Scott tried to insist that they travel somewhere, Julie refused to go along. She felt that starting a family would be the natural evolution of their relationship.

So how do couples like Scott and Julie handle a situation when compromise seems to fail with the natural evolution of a relationship? Some people try bullying their partner into seeing things their way. Others simply do nothing and hope that time will heal their wounds, or at least, that the problem might go away.

In either case, an odd, two-sided logic seems to prevail: *When my partner goes along with my choice, it's a sign of intimacy, compromise, and togetherness. However, when my partner asserts his or her choice, it's an unhealthy sign of control and perhaps even lack of love.*

In a sense, a person caught in this paradigm expects the impossible: absolute agreement and togetherness, along with complete honesty from his or her partner.

Dr. David Schnarch refers to this situation as the two-choice dilemma. In essence, it's the fantasy couples employ when one person wants two opposing choices at the same time, for example, the desire for greater financial stability along with the desire to avoid sacrifice and hard work. Unless you're one of the lucky few to win the lottery, odds are you're only going to get one of the two.

Most people try to avoid these dilemmas at first, preferring to fantasize that they can have it all. Sure, John loves Jane and ranks his marriage as being perhaps the most important relationship in his life. However he's on the fence about having children. Jane wants kids, but whenever she brings up the issue, John finds an excuse to delay the discussion.

In John's fantasy, he is married and childless. Sure, he can have this, but only at the expense of his wife's happiness.

Those of us with a weak sense of self and low differentiation will do whatever we can to stay within the comfort of our fantasies. This might include sabotaging our partners' efforts to make choices that go against our desires. Fortunately or unfortunately, there comes a time when the status quo becomes intolerable to one person in the relationship. This is when things can, and often do, get ugly.

So, if Jane wants children, she's going to have to confront her two-choice dilemma:

1. Stay with John and not have children.

2. Leave John for someone who wants children.

The fantasy is now shattered: She can no longer live with the status quo of staying married to John and having a peaceful, happy relationship without children.

Facing choices like these might seem grim, and I can imagine you're thinking, as many clients do when faced with the reality of their choices, that neither one looks particularly palatable. But perhaps that's exactly the point. This process can help us confront the worst in us, to allow the best in us to shine through.

In John's case, he has two options, both very difficult: he can be honest with himself, and with Jane, about his unwillingness to have kids, or he can choose to stay with Jane and have children. If he chooses the latter, it will probably be because he's confronted his own issues and decided that his ambivalence had more to do with anxiety about parenthood than with actually not wanting children. Once he's consciously made this choice, there's actually a really good chance the couple will stay together, build a family, and grow personally along the way. In fact, I have seen this exact scenario play out with my clients more than a few times.

Whatever the core issue, these two-choice dilemmas require partners to choose between the lesser of two evils: either continue to compromise, requiring each person in the relationship to sacrifice in an attempt to keep their partners calm and content; or face the uncertainty and anxiety of confronting their own issues and their partner's anxiety.

Working through two-choice dilemmas is anything but pretty. From the start, the screaming, accusations, lying, and game playing can make anyone wonder: What bad karma did these two incur to end up with each other? Indeed, my clients often look at other couples and turn to me to ask "No one else goes through this, why us?"

But two-choice dilemmas are a natural part of all long-term relationships. It's just that most of us do such a good job at hiding the ugly parts of our marriage to outsiders that many couples think they're the only ones with problems.

The good news is that, if these two-choice dilemmas are handled with maturity, they can help both people find clarity about what they really want in life.

Look at these difficult situations as a gift: offering couples the exciting opportunity to break through their own inertia and residual childhood neuroses. Our relationship problems actually provide the impetus to break free from fusion, and help create space for each other to have real choice. And with choice comes freedom — one of the greatest gifts we can give to those we love.

2.4 Fighting fusion: being your own person

Consider these statements:

- I need to be my own person.
- Take me as I am.
- I need to leave this relationship to find out who I really am.
- I can't bear to be without you.
- You complete me.

What do all these statements have in common? They all express the unhealthy dependence called "fusion."

Because people with low differentiation have trouble separating their own thoughts and feelings from those they're close to, they tend to take on their partners' anxieties. Just think of the example I gave earlier: If I pinch your mom, do you scream, "Ow!"? What if I pinch your partner?

Fusion is yet another emotional legacy we inherit from our family of origin. In highly fused families, members play specific roles, and learn how to speak, listen, and bite their tongues for the sake of harmony, or to avoid punishment. Conformity keeps anxious feelings at bay, and creates the illusion that everyone's getting along just fine.

In many people's minds, the concepts of fusion and love have become hopelessly intertwined. Over the course of a typical work week, I hear partners tell each other endless variations of the quotes you saw at the beginning of this chapter. The general message is: *When I'm around you, I feel uneasy and I need something to be different — from you or from myself — to make me feel better.*

Depending on how you witnessed these uneasy experiences being handled in your family growing up, you may resort to one of two types of needs, either needing your partner to do something to make you feel better or needing to find some distance from him or her.

The goal of the first: We expect our partners to make us feel more calm, confident, sexy, intelligent ... like all-around special people in their lives. Most people view this process as a natural part of love and committed relationships. But what about the second case, when this extreme dependence drives people to distance themselves from those with whom they're supposed to be closest? These two reactions may seem like opposites, but they're actually flip sides of the same fusion coin.

People who pride themselves on their independence often proclaim their autonomy as Popeye does: "I yam what I yam and that's all what I yam."

In our society, we're taught to think of independence and maturity as pretty much the same thing, but in fact this unhealthy autonomy can also be a sign of the opposite. People who struggle with commitment often do so out of fear of losing themselves to that commitment, be it a career, relationship, or long-term project. According to Dr. David Schnarch, because of their fragile sense of self they are "fearful of disappearing in a relationship and do things to avoid their partner's emotional engulfment."

These individuals may express their autonomy with the noblest of intentions, for example, by leaving their families to meditate in an ashram. But in truth, they're only able to relax and feel calm and clear-headed when they are far from their families. Behavior like this screams, I'm independent, I don't need anybody!

Alas, I think, when I hear these stories, "thou doth protest too much"; this insistence on independence signifies profound fusion, on an unhealthy level.

Now that we've seen that fusion can work in these two ways, we can also start to visualize how these two processes — extreme dependence and extreme withdrawal — affect how we end up choosing our partners in some pretty obvious ways.

2.5 Pursuers and Distancers

> "I enjoyed the chase."
>
> — Rod Stewart

As we've seen, fusion — extreme emotional dependence — can act paradoxically, and often plays out as one partner either pursuing or distancing himself or herself from the other.

A pursuer is the person in the relationship who seeks contact and feels insecure and anxious when he or she feels like a partner is more distant. When he or she feels too much distance from a partner he or she will do anything to bridge the distance. This might take the form of nagging or criticizing, or creating drama to keep the other close. As you can imagine, pursuers fall into the category of people who tend to conform in order to calm their insecurities.

A distancer, on the other hand, tends to assert his or her own autonomy in order to alleviate anxieties. Distancers will often go to great lengths to portray this distancing as a sign of independence, insisting on having separate friends, hobbies, or apartments. He or she might blame the partner for making him or her need to establish that distance, for example, by telling the partner he or she is too needy.

These two personality types can create an unpleasant, vicious cycle. When a pursuer pursues a distancer, the distancer feels increasingly suffocated and increases the detachment. This, in turn, causes the pursuer to push harder. This kind of unhealthy cycle can be very difficult to break.

So why do pursuers often choose distancers, and vice versa?

This, too, comes back to differentiation. We tend to choose partners at the same level of differentiation as ourselves, but with opposing coping mechanisms. So pursuers and distancers choose each other because this is the pattern of emotional functioning that they are used to.

At the beginning of your relationship, you may not see how this dynamic plays out. But over time, as major decisions need to be made and compromise starts to take a back seat to their real desires, people regress to their basic mode of functioning: some variation of pushing for more closeness or fleeing for cover. And so the dance, as we therapists like to call it, begins.

This also explains why one partner in a relationship is often viewed by others — as well as by the couple — as more emotionally mature than the other partner. But looks are usually deceiving. If you peek behind the scenes, you might discover that both partners are emotionally well-suited for one another. Let's look at an example to see how this works.

> As far back as Jack can remember, he kept his feelings to himself; more so when he is feeling stressed or anxious. Jack's partner Susan can also get stressed out. However, while Jack copes by closing in on himself, Susan responds by dramatizing her emotions to anyone who will listen. Most people assume that Jack is calm and mature, unfazed by pressure, and that Susan is the emotionally volatile half of the couple. In reality, they're both sensitive to stress; Susan's is just more outwardly visible, while Jack gives a false impression of his ability to cope.

So now we have a clue that can help us answer that age-old question: "Am I with the right person?"

All too often, in my office, I sit with pursuers and distancers who come in convinced they're with the wrong person. They figure (wrongly) that they'd fit better with someone who responds to emotion and anxiety in the same way they do, but nothing could be further from the truth. These opposing coping mechanisms aren't a sign of dysfunction, but rather, the type of personality most complementary to our own.

Part of the reason for this is that we choose people at the same maturity level (or level of differentiation) as ourselves. It seems like we have a built-in emotional screening process that weeds out people who are either too mature or immature. Given enough attraction and commonalities, we will generally choose the right person for our emotional temperament.

Most people don't like to hear this. It just doesn't seem fair: how could their freedom of choice be hijacked in this way by their family histories?

To a degree, it's true — we don't have control over our earliest childhood assumptions about relationships. However, that doesn't mean we're stuck right now, in the present. We don't have to be slaves to our family history. It is possible to change within our current relationships, learning to remain calm in the face of powerful emotions and anxieties.

The end result is progress: higher differentiation and less pursuing or distancing. Ultimately, this lets us choose a more mature partner, and step off the rollercoaster dynamic of pursuing and distancing.

3. The (Naturally) Dark Side of Relationships

> *"You ain't that tall, you got heels on, your lips ain't that big, you had Botox, your eyes ain't that color, you got them contacts in, your hair ain't ... "*
>
> — Chris Rock, *Liars*

The other day, I overheard two guys in their early twenties talking in the gym locker room. The conversation went like this:

- **Guy 1:** Should I take her to a movie then dinner, or a dinner and then a movie?

- **Guy 2:** Definitely start with a dinner, and then a movie.

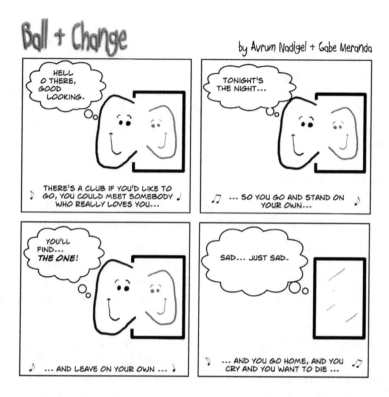

- **Guy 1:** Yeah, I guess. I don't want to mess this up, I really like this girl.

- **Guy 2:** I'm telling you, start with dinner, then the movie. Trust me.

If I had more courage, I would have liked to approach Guy 2 and asked him what he thought would happen if Guy 1 started with a movie. What irreparable damage would be done if popcorn preceded pasta?

While not all trivial matters are overanalyzed to this ridiculous degree, dating does expose our vulnerabilities, wishes, and fears, laying them bare to the world. That's part of what I think of as the (naturally) dark side of committed relationships. This section will deal mainly with the theoretical side, looking at what our vulnerabilities are. The next chapters will look constructively at changing our responses to these adverse conditions so they don't have to be dealbreakers.

To get even more specific, dating reveals our need for companionship and sexual intimacy, as well as the potential for winding up alone and rejected. All of these feelings can be stirred up on a single date.

For some, the need to be liked and loved is so profound they will describe the encounter with great intensity. They spend a lot of time trying to second guess what the person sitting across from them is thinking and feeling. But because they don't know the person (yet), cues are misread, heightening stress. This, of course, creates a perfect storm in which people lose themselves temporarily to the fogginess of their anxiety and stress. They find themselves agreeing with ideas they might never have considered when in a calmer state: "Sure, I'm open to moving to a small town while you complete a six-year post-doctoral program ... Did I just say that?"

I've heard many stories of clients who have lost themselves, creating foreseeable problems in this haze of early dating and courtship.

In one couple, the wife accused her husband of lying about wanting children. "On our first date," she insisted, "he told me how much he loved children and how he looked forward to having a large family." He said, "Yes, at the time I did think I wanted those things. Now I think differently."

When we met alone, he confided to me that he had never wanted children, but knew she'd never have agreed to a second date if he'd revealed the truth. "Back then," he continued, "I hid myself from anyone who was important to me. I was petrified of being alone. Truthfully, back then, I had no idea what I wanted. So when someone asked me what I thought about this or that issue, I'd try to give them the answer that I thought they were looking for."

Early on, couples plant the seeds for these future problems because:

- They don't want to cause problems in the early stages of a fun dating experience, influenced more by feelings than principles, as we've discussed already.

- They don't create the opportunities to learn about the character of the person they are dating. In the next section, I will address the issue of character, and how you can plan dates to ensure you're getting to know the deeper parts of potential partners.

- They get caught up in their fears and anxieties, and do their best to hide the undesirable parts of themselves to stave off being alone.

3.1 Matching your emotional maturity

> *"We accept the love we think we deserve."*
>
> — Stephen Chbosky, *The Perks of Being a Wallflower*

Every once in a while, on a regular publishing-industry schedule, a self-help relationship or growth book is released which purports to have the answer as to why you're miserable and are (fill in your current status: single, dating, married, etc.). One of these books, which later morphed into a movie and then a movement, was called *He's Just Not That Into You*.

It did its best to instruct the masses, with the help of quasi-marine corps drill sergeant instructions like "You picked a lemon, throw it away, lemonade is overrated," and "You already have one asshole. You don't need another." Sure, they're great one-liners, but beneath it all, the book's writers echoed a popular, though faulty, idea: If you're not getting what you want or not being treated right, it's your partner's fault. The onus is on you to get back out there and choose better next time.

If only it were that easy. The fallacy of the book's premise lies in the fact that most people don't actually change what type of partner they choose, despite past failures. Instead, for reasons we've explored in this and previous chapters, they pick similar partners over and over again.

The most important similarity that can come back to haunt us in relationship after relationship is one of emotional development.

Because we choose partners who are at the same level of differentiation, emotional maturity, and psychological health as ourselves, explains *New York Times*-bestselling relationship expert Maggie Scarf, it's easy to see how emotional functioning is passed down from generation to generation. Scarf writes in her book *Intimate Partners*: "... the relatively undifferentiated person will select a spouse who is equally fused to his or her family of origin (equally sane or equally crazy). It is probable, moreover, that these poorly differentiated people, now a marital couple, will themselves become highly fused and will produce a family with the same characteristics (a bunch of sane kids or a bunch of crazy kids)."

But how does all this play out in the context of dating? Suppose you're on a date where something just seems off about the other person (who hasn't been in that situation?). Hard as you try, you can't get past a general uneasiness with how this person makes you feel.

According to differentiation theory, this usually happens when you're with someone who is lower than you in differentiation but, more interestingly, it can also occur with someone who is higher than you. So, with a person lower on the scale, you might find them too emotional, or not stable enough. If they're on the higher end of the differentiation scale, you might deem them not spirited enough, too boring. According to Schnarch, "If partners are not at the same level of differentiation, the relationship usually breaks up early."

What does he mean by early? Basically, you'll know earlier in the relationship if you're with the wrong person by that disquieting thought of not being "completed" in some way. When I was single, this idea was very comforting: "Ah, not all 365,000 women are a potential match for me."

Of course, the question becomes, how can you tip the scales in your favor to meet the right match? Differentiation theory can help.

Before I heard of differentiation theory, I was perplexed by my disinterest in women who were deemed excellent catches by friends and family. On paper, these women were ideal in many ways; they were attractive, and we had similar interests. But we were miles apart in one important area: their differentiation levels far exceeded my own.

Not unlike wearing a suit that is two sizes two small, it simply didn't feel right to me. The more I tried to force the connection — doing my best to avoid letting a good one slip away — the more unattractive the relationship became. I usually figured this was a byproduct of my fear of commitment. But over time, I came to appreciate the elegance of differentiation theory as a screening tool to avoid prolonging relationships with people who were simply incompatible with me on that level.

You can use the concept of differentiation to become a more discerning evaluator of prospective mates by understanding your own level of emotional maturity.

3.2 Too many fish?

> "As the number of choices keeps growing, negative aspects of having a multitude of options begin to appear. At this point, choice no longer liberates, but debilitates. It might even be said to tyrannize."
>
> — Dr. Barry Schwartz, *The Paradox of Choice*

Meet Jim. Jim is in his late twenties and just ended a serious relationship. He doesn't want to waste another three years of his life with the wrong woman. Thinking aloud about his past relationship, Jim recalls the warning signs and problems that, in retrospect, he now thinks should have alerted him to being in the wrong relationship. He's certain he chose the wrong partner last time and is adamant that he won't make the same mistake again next time. So he signs up for an online dating site hoping to find as many women as possible, to see who's the best fit. He confidently declares, "The more options, the more likely it is that I'm going to find my life partner."

Having read all you have so far about differentiation and fusion, and seen the mistakes made by couples in the examples, you may have started to realize that unless he's made concrete changes, not much will be different for Jim next time around. And unfortunately for Jim, many studies suggest that the number of choices are actually an impediment, not an advantage, when looking for a life partner. Psychologist Barry Schwartz, well-known for his TED talk on the subject of choice, writes: "Choice overload can make you question the decisions you make before you even make them, it can set you up for unrealistically high expectations, and it can make you blame yourself for any and all failures. In the long run, this can lead to decision-making paralysis. And in a culture that tells us that there is no excuse for falling short of perfection when your options are limitless, too much choice can lead to clinical depression."

The problem's even thornier for people who fear making the wrong choice in a life partner. Searching for the ideal, each flaw in a date leads these people back to the Internet, to page after page of fresh singles to connect with. It's a self-fulfilling prophecy: you enter the date anxious about choosing the wrong partner, so you're hyper-vigilant about any physical or psychological blemish. I've talked to people who get home from an Internet date and go right onto the computer to compare the date to other prospects (c'mon, admit it, we've all done it!). Of course, it's inevitable that they'll find someone "better," which then accentuates any "defects" they found in that night's date. That's how dating profiles work, of course: they're an advertisement, showing the best side of a person (if not the most honest side) and hiding the imperfections we all have.

But if more choice gives you less freedom, then you can use what you now know about differentiation theory to your advantage in two important ways:

First, you no longer have to be overwhelmed by the sheer number of profiles to wade through on an online dating site. As I hope you've seen through my own story, when you can function better — with less reactivity and a greater awareness of your principles, passions, and values — in any of your relationships, this helps all of your relationships. The better you get at this, the easier it will be to paint a picture of what your ideal mate will look like: his or her life goals, and principles. At that point, your online dating searches will be more refined, and your blind dates a little less blind. With an attraction based on values and principles, you'll avoid disastrous dates, and maybe even start enjoying the dating process.

Second, any efforts you make to increase your level of differentiation will result in more mature relationships, giving you a greater likelihood of increased pleasure and fewer difficulties in connecting.

In other words, rather than focusing outwardly by scouring the Internet for hours looking for the perfect mate, you could better spend those hours looking inwardly at yourself.

We've all heard the saying "Know Thyself." The goal is to make that a reality. With clearer thinking about what you will and won't stand for in a relationship, you'll be better equipped to create an online dating profile that attracts genuinely potential mates, with less time wasted on all sides.

3.3 Warming up those cold feet

> *"Some men are born with cold feet; some acquire cold feet; and some have cold feet thrust upon them."*
>
> — Anonymous

> *"Nobody's ready for marriage; marriage makes you ready for marriage."*
>
> — Dr. David Schnarch, *Passionate Marriage*

A few weeks before my wedding, I bumped into a female friend on the street. The last time we'd seen each other, a few years prior, we had both been single. I told her that I was engaged. She countered with, "I'm dating someone, but I'm having a really tough time with the relationship."

I sat back and waited for the usual laundry list of what was wrong with her partner, or with men in general. Instead, she focused on herself: "I'm in my mid-thirties, and while I know myself better than before, I'm pretty set in my ways. I'm finding it really hard to create space for someone. In my twenties, everyone told me to figure stuff out before you get married, but now I'm not so sure that if that advice was correct. Do you get any of this?"

Yes, I thought, *more than you can imagine.*

Like my friend, I had always thought that by working on myself, I'd be ready for the commitment of being in a long-term relationship. So I worked on improving myself through therapy and traveling the world. Guess what? It didn't work.

I now believe that many people I knew at the time who prolonged emotional commitment in the name of building self-awareness were actually running scared. The meditation retreats, career changes, and rebranding of self weren't harmful in and of themselves. However, if those friends were asked when they intended to settle down, their answer was usually: "Oh, not yet. I've got too much to do. I don't nearly have enough of (some imagined thing that was lacking — money, home, job stability, emotional health, etc.), to get married yet."

Don't get me wrong, I'm not saying self-growth and maturity don't help us in our relationships. However, I have come to appreciate that running from anxiety only creates more anxiety. Even therapy can be a way to avoid things that increase our anxiety and make us feel uneasy.

One reason some people develop cold feet as adults is that they grew up in families where they were completely in tune with the needs of their parents and siblings. Along the way, they lost track of themselves, their own interests, and identities. Psychoanalyst Alice Miller refers to these children as "gifted." She believes they have an inborn sensitivity to others' suffering, and are raised into their family role of helping those in need. However, this gift comes at a price: an underdeveloped true self. They become chameleons and helpers, always on the lookout for what others need, and what others think of them.

As adults, these gifted people often crumble under the weight of intimacy in their relationships. Whatever self they have been able to cultivate — often in their twenties or thirties — is too fragile to risk losing to the perceived demands of a love relationship. These people wince when told it takes compromise to make a relationship work. And wince they should! They know more than anyone that chronically sacrificing yourself for others leaves you feeling empty.

Unfortunately, this strategy of avoiding compromise all too often leaves them alone. Or they may become serial daters or turn to promiscuity to avoid intimacy and long-term relationships that would demand compromise. Whatever the case, they've side-stepped the need to make a commitment.

As I met with clients who were a little too exuberant about their promiscuity and need to play the field, I came to realize that they were the ones desperately afraid they wouldn't find love, or that they'd lose themselves in a relationship. Whatever the case, most of their relationship decisions were driven not by confidence but by fear. Their paralysis when it comes to closeness impacts everything they do.

Many of my clients express fears about falling into a bad marriage. They've all seen married couples who are clearly bored and have nothing to say to each other, or who bicker and hold deep resentment. They fear divorce and the possibility of fighting over assets and the custody of children.

I can relate to this, and it's not entirely unwarranted, given the statistics. Thinking of myself in my early thirties, with my difficulties committing to women, I'd get a panicky, claustrophobic feeling whenever my partner tried to discuss the future. I'd respond by focusing on her flaws, which, of course, I was ready to identify with lightning speed and precision. As a relationship progressed, I told myself these flaws were warning signs that proved to me that I was in the wrong relationship.

But over time, I started being able to identify how this fear of commitment drove me to discover those flaws — real and imagined — in my partners. They'd compel me to end relationships, and avoid having to deal with the more primal anxiety related to long-term commitment. Once I understood this process, it was easier to focus on strategies to stay with the anxiety (and relationship) versus running away.

Maybe you can't really relate to this story. Perhaps you're the type who firmly believes in the old adage that "when you're with the right person, you'll just know." When you perceive a flaw, you feel like you must listen closely to the feelings that something's wrong with the relationship. That's certainly true some of the time, but often that sense of being with the right person is simply wrong.

I've worked with too many divorced clients who, when they first met their ex-spouse, were sure they were with the right person. Some were high school sweethearts; others succumbed to love at first sight. I've also worked with couples who started their relationship with a lot of ambiguity about their choice of mate, and ended up creating a deep and loving relationship.

How can we know when going with our gut is the best thing to do?

According to Dr. Schnarch, picking a partner often happens for the wrong reasons I've already mentioned: our partner makes us feel complete, helps us feel validated and good about ourselves, or alleviates our anxieties. But believe it or not, picking a partner for the wrong reasons doesn't always mean the relationship is doomed.

Schnarch states that in this kind of situation, "We haven't matured enough for right reasons to exist yet. Struggling with wrong reasons for getting married can produce right reasons to stay married." Which is yet another reason why self-improvement when you're single can be extremely helpful, but it won't prepare you for a healthy long-term relationship as much as doing the work while in a long-term relationship. Paradox, huh?

I suggest that you view the anxiety that comes with making a commitment as natural, and that you (slowly!) learn to endure that anxiety. This is sort of like building up your tolerance, so you can learn to stick with the commitment, rather than flee. This is a crucial point: Anxiety begets anxiety, so the best way to alleviate your cold feet is to ride out the fear.

Put another way, there's no greater fear than fear itself.

In a chapter full of paradoxes, here, then, is one last one: even relationships which feel wrong may wind up being the best relationships in which to grow and mature into the best version of yourself. I have worked with successful couples who, with a bit of embarrassment, claim they got married for all the wrong reasons. Yet, they were able to turn these wrong reasons around, using the struggles this inevitably brought to sharpen their focus on what they value, and the way they want to live their lives.

This is also true in all areas of life, whether career, romance or religion. In time, and with work, your wrong reasons give way to right and solid reasons. If you're truly devoted to improving yourself individually, the best advice along your path to a healthy, creative self is to hitch yourself to the "people-growing" machine of a committed relationship.

3.4 Communication issues

> "Relationship difficulties are often not about an inability to 'communicate.' Communication is no virtue if you can't stand the message."
>
> — Dr. David Schnarch, *Passionate Marriage*

Where did you live as a teenager? Try to actually visualize it. Picture your home: the entranceway, the living room, and the kitchen. Now, picture an average supper time in your home. Who's sitting at the table? Where are your parents? What are they talking about? Gossip? Religious ideas? Concerns about the children? Do they look at each other or is one busy while the other one is talking? As you picture this scene, is it a good memory? Do you feel happy? Are you bored? Angry? Sad? Scared?

One last question: Is this the type of rapport you hope to have with your partner?

When I introduce this exercise in a large group, most of the audience will wince as memories become clear. Comments range from: "My parents simply co-existed. I have hard time understanding what they saw in each other," to "When they talked, their statements came out like accusations."

My next question is generally, "What could your parents do to improve their dynamic?" The answer is amazingly consistent: "They need to improve how they communicate."

Most of us would be tempted to name communication problems as the main cause of relationship difficulties. We figure: If my partner would listen better and take into consideration my struggles, wounds, and wishes, he or she would have more compassion for what I'm saying, and then we wouldn't fight so much.

On the surface this sounds reasonable. Yet I've observed many couples who could communicate quite clearly with each other, yet were neither getting their needs met, nor feeling fulfilled in the relationship.

So why do we put so much time and effort into fixing communication if there's no guarantee that it will help our relationship? For decades now, well-meaning relationship experts have offered books, workshops, and videos designed to help couples improve communication. And yet we're often no better at listening and empathizing with our partners than our grandparents were (and our grandparents had little or no professional guidance on communicating with their spouses!).

Indeed, when it comes to issues fraught with tension and potential conflict, we're often no further ahead — for all the latest books, lectures and techniques — than our grandparents were at our age.

Since these often focus on communication and other behavioral tips and tricks that we've dealt with already, these tools tend to obscure the truth. Marriages break down because partners lack the maturity to stand on their own two feet, soothe their own sensitivities, and give themselves and their partners the space for healthy differences of opinion. Compromise feels good (in the moment), but ultimately stunts maturity and growth.

Neither compromise nor communication by itself is the answer.

Clients are often distraught when they hear their non-communicative partners expressing themselves openly to friends. Bafflingly, the partner can't explain why communication is so easy under other circumstances: "I just feel comfortable talking to him (or her)." (Interestingly, the people they feel most comfortable with are rarely family members or a spouse.)

Clearly, if your partner can listen and empathize with friends, he or she is not lacking in communication skills. That's why it feels so personal: it seems like it's less about communication, and more about your mate's ability or desire to talk to you.

According to Schnarch in *Passionate Marriage*, couples don't have trouble communicating; they simply can't stand the message. Moreover, he believes that lack of communication is often just the opposite: "If you truly can't communicate' you wouldn't know that you don't want to hear what your partner has to say. The silence of married couples is testimony to their good communication each spouse knows the other doesn't want to hear what's on his or her mind!"

So when do we see this so-called lack of communication happening most? In any relationship where we care too much about what the other person thinks of us, or believe the other person doesn't think very highly of us.

It happens all the time between teenagers and their parents. A father becomes worried about a situation but is unable to control the outcome. He repeats his message over and over until his teenage son says, "Uh-huh, uh-huh." To which the father explodes with," 'Uh-huh' is not communication!"

Both the teenager and the parent would probably agree that they can't communicate. But they'd be wrong: they're both communicating just fine! You just have to look at what messages are being sent and received.

The teenager is saying: "Dad, I can't talk to you, because whenever I try I get a lecture. You get so worked up about everything that all I can do for you is try to be good, and stay away from the house." While the father is saying: "I love you, but I don't trust you. The world is a scary place and I'm having trouble letting go. If you were eight, I'd keep you at home. But I can't, and I can't begin to fathom what I'd do if something bad happened to you."

Schnarch believes that the problem in loving relationships isn't too little communication, it's that people don't know how to stop communicating. Anxiety and neediness keep pushing us to demand that our partners soothe us by telling us what we want to hear, despite years of clear signals that they either can't or don't want to play that role.

We also want a guarantee that our mate won't say or do something that will make us more upset. As you've probably already imagined, this is an unsustainable dynamic if either partner wants to feel fulfilled in a mature relationship. According to Schnarch, couples who are unable to work through this impasse often separate and divorce in what he calls "misguided attempts to halt the exchange of information. When I know you truly think I'm a jerk, we have good communication — but that doesn't mean we feel like talking!"

In the early stages of a relationship, both partners learn quickly what each other's sensitivities are. Driven to avoid painful feelings, we often learn to avoid discussing subjects that raise anxiety or ill feelings within our partner. On the other hand, when people think of good communication, they're often referring to messages that reinforce how they want to be perceived. Schnarch continues: "We don't communicate" is code for "I refuse to accept that message — send me a different one! How dare you see me [or the issue] that way!"

When they don't get what they need to hear, partners zone out on their iPhones or play with their soup … any activity that lets them hide their true feelings and opinions from their spouses.

Efforts to improve communication, whether by taking a class or reading a self-help book, can't help people who simply don't want to hear their partner's message. However, this status quo of silence and contempt is obviously not sustainable.

So what can you do?

Make a focused effort to get clear about what you believe and think. That, in and of itself, is quite a task; a big step for many people. The next step is trying to live according to your principles and beliefs, and being prepared for the consequences. The better you can do this in front of the people you care about most — without screaming, caving in, or cutting off conversation — the stronger your backbone will become.

In time, you'll find that you don't need your partner, friends, parents, or colleagues to take care of you; you won't need them to always agree with your ideas. You will have learned not to confuse a difference of opinion with a lack of love.

At this point, you might be thinking: "Well, you don't know my partner! If I told him what I was really thinking, he'd get really quiet, and then angry, and even contemplate leaving the relationship. We have three kids, and I have no interest in being a single mom."

We all have our reasons (read: fears) for keeping things the same. Though I've found that, in my own life and for many of my clients, few of these fears are grounded in reality. We need to be honest with ourselves. Are we really not walking the walk because of some scary thing lurking out there, or are we nurturing our fear of the unknown? Only you can answer this for yourself.

So yes, it is more difficult to live according to our values and to ask directly for things that we want and don't want. However, if the only alternative is a stale, lifeless relationship, then the answer, though tough, is clear. Each position comes with its own consequences, however, only one can lead towards rich and loving long-term relationships.

3.5 Jealousy and external threats

> "I've never been the jealous type, so I don't understand why I'm so bothered by your platonic relationship with Cathy."
>
> "This is totally crazy — I'm not even attracted to Cathy."
>
> "You say that, but ... "

If I don't intervene in conversations like these, I've seen the back-and-forth accusations and justifications go on *ad infinitum*. Often, I'll interrupt the cycle by saying, "You know, you can do this for free at home. Which one of you is able to pull yourself out of this tug of war?" Too frequently, a couple is too tangled up in the web of jealousy to hear what I'm saying.

What's the biggest source of jealousy these days? It's no surprise that where jealousy plays out most often is on the Internet, usually in the form of pornography and online chatting. As we all know, pornography is everywhere, at our fingertips 24/7. As well, meeting someone new or reconnecting with an old friend and creating an online flirtation is so simple we've almost all done it. Today's therapists are deluged with clients who come to see them upon discovering their partner's covert online life. Sometimes, it's not even covert: the partner doesn't bother to hide his or her porn surfing or Internet dalliance.

This book is not focused on the ethics (or lack thereof) of Internet sexual activities. But the jealousy that ensues can be a factor in any relationship. As with non-computerized erotica, the lower one's level of differentiation, the more likely he or she will experience the other's pornography or sex-laced chats as a violation or betrayal. This is because it greatly threatens his or her reflected sense of self, identity, and security. Using the Internet for sexual stimulation or emotional affairs is especially corrosive to relationships built on the shaky foundation of emotional fusion, which includes, unfortunately, far too many marriages.

If you rely on your partner to "complete" you, to make you feel worthy, attractive, and lovable, then any threat to your relationship will be too much to bear. You need to maintain a feeling of togetherness in order to maintain your equilibrium. When your relationship is solid, you feel solid. But when imagined or real problems come to the fore, you muster forces, ready to defend and attack at a moment's notice. The idea of your relationship ending might make you feel jittery, anxious, and lost. Some experience the loss of their relationship as the loss of themselves: a profoundly frightening thought.

When people lack internal stability — a strong sense of self and self-esteem — they rely heavily on their relationships for stability and meaning. When that's the case, they are vulnerable to feeling destabilized by internal or external anxiety. Some people react to this instability by trying to get closer to their partners, either physically or emotionally. But this kind of move can make the problem worse, because it frequently triggers a counter-reaction as their partners withdraw from the closeness. According to family therapist Roberta M. Gilbert, when this happens, the pursuer, seeking more closeness and togetherness, can become very jealous, fearing their partner's distance is due to an affair, or that he/she is unlovable.

That isn't to say the distancing partner isn't playing an important part in the jealousy dance. Often, he or she too will try and use the therapy hour with me to justify a position, arguing, "I'm only doing this as an act of maturity and independence." If he or she truly wants to end the negative cycle, he or she must stop the distancing in response to their partner's bid for intimacy. The person needs to adopt healthier ways of self-soothing and staying with intimacy, instead of needing to run away.

The jealous partner, who seeks more assurances and closeness, might say to me, "I simply love and care for my partner too deeply." But if the person wants to break out of this destructive dynamic, he or she will need to discover his or her own true self-worth, separate from what the relationship or partner provides.

In time, as he or she learns to give himself or herself what is needed he or she will feel less compelled to turn to a partner for these things. This space and freedom will provide both partners with more choice in terms of how they respond to real or imagined threats.

4. Why Sexual Intimacy Fails

> *"Personally I know nothing about sex because I've always been married."*
>
> — Zsa Zsa Gabor

I usually shop in one of two grocery stores. Both border communities with a large concentration of Orthodox Jews. Out of respect for the community's modesty laws and customs, the stores have designated family-friendly aisles, where magazines with racy photos and subject matter are removed. The magazines displayed in the regular aisles are not pornographic; they tend to be more oriented towards fashion and sports. Yet each cover tends to teeter on the brink of soft porn. One popular trend is sexual advice lists, such as "10 Tips to Bring Your Partner to His Ultimate Orgasm!" What this has to do with fitness or fashion is lost on me. The advice is almost always technical, focusing on techniques and "secrets" that promise readers more and better sex with their partners.

If we believe these magazines, their readers are simply ill-informed about how to touch their partner (or themselves). If they could just learn these techniques, their sexual problems would be over. The cover stories suggest we're simply lacking in information about sex, but, in fact, nothing could be further from the truth.

For many of us, sex education started in elementary school, and continued throughout high school. In university, students are bombarded with information on how to have safe and good sex. And let's not forget Google, the portal to a world of sexually explicit material, in any format you desire. Given the plethora of information about sex, why do jokes still make their way into comedy routines? How come low sexual desire and other sexual problems are still with us, even with all these experts sharing their secrets?

I believe there are three reasons for this:

1. There is a natural ebb and flow to sexual relationships, particularly in long-term relationships.

2. The faulty assumption that good sex is a natural byproduct of healthy monogamous relationships.

3. These tips tend to focus on techniques and tools rather than the underlying, emotionally-driven forces that pull people apart. A vibrator is of little use to people who are too anxious to hug, kiss, and tackle difficult conversations.

4.1 Relationships ebb and flow

There is a natural ebb and flow to sexual relationships, particularly in long-term relationships. Imagine you're standing in a dining hall facing a large buffet of food. Cupcakes of different sizes and color adorn the tables: chocolate frosting with sprinkles, vanilla cream with espresso beans. The sight itself excites your imagination about what that first bite will taste like. You dig in to your first cupcake. The combination of vanilla frosting and chocolate cake have your tongue doing somersaults. But as you hit your third cake, all the delight has faded to sawdust. You flag down the caterer ... what you want is real food.

YOU: These cupcakes are delicious, but I'm wondering if you'll be serving anything else?

CATERER: I don't understand; you just said you loved cupcakes.

YOU: I do, I do, but perhaps a salad?

CATERER: You can make salad at home; it's easy.

YOU: How about a main course; steak, perhaps?

CATERER: Have you ever seen a slaughterhouse?

YOU: Okay, soup. Any chance for soup?

CATERER: No can do. I served soup once before, and a guest burned himself. Hefty lawsuit. Never again.

You soon head home, hungry and bored, wondering how it was possible that only a couple of hours ago those cupcakes tasted so delicious.

Sex with a new partner is a lot like those first few bites of your first cupcake. The sights and smells are enticing; your imagination conjures up rich previews about what the experience will be like. And those first few bites, well, those may be even better than the fantasy. Sadly, just as soon as the thrill began, it's gone. Such is the nature of novelty: What is new, dangerous and exciting is bound to become routine over time.

According to Dr. Schnarch, that's just how committed relationships should function. Moreover, he argues that one of the main reasons sexual arousal wanes is because of what each partner doesn't want to do. Schnarch writes: "Sexual relationships always consist of leftovers - you get to decide what you don't want to do. I get to decide what I don't want to do, and we do whatever's left over."

In the beginning, these "leftover" sexual acts are often enough to satiate sexual appetites. Which is why it's so baffling and disheartening for couples when these same behaviors soon result in boredom. Here's an example.

> Stephanie and Mark had been dating for a few weeks. After a romantic night of good food, and copious amounts of wine, Mark asked Stephanie if she'd like to go back to his apartment. Stephanie said, "Yes, but we need to talk."

Amid adrenaline and fear, she bravely shared her vulnerability. "This has nothing to do with you," she began tentatively, "but I'm not comfortable performing oral sex."

Mark was so thrilled to pursue any physical intimacy that he responded, "No problem; I'd never pressure you to do anything you don't want to do." He then added, "Actually, it's probably a good time to mention that I prefer to sleep alone. I mean, you can stay over, we can have breakfast and spend the day together, but I'd prefer to sleep alone in my bed."

Like Mark, Stephanie accepted Mark's condition easily; she just wanted things to continue moving forward."I totally understand," she said. "Now that we've gotten that out of the way, let's pay the bill and get out of here!"

Later in the relationship, when natural boredom encroaches, it's especially difficult for those who are lower on the scale of differentiation. Because they rely on their partners to help them feel good and sexy, any request for change, or admission of boredom, will result in hurt feelings. Problems can go from bad to worse as each partner starts assigning blame. They may attack: "You were fine with the way I kissed when we first met!" Or they may turn it back onto themselves: "I knew it. I was never good at oral sex." Or they may disparage the entire relationship: "Things shouldn't be this way. I picked the wrong person."

When it comes to sexual relationships, the stereotype is generally true: these difficulties commonly emerge when a couple has a child, especially their first. Life changes drastically, and typically the mother (although this happens to new dads as well) becomes less interested in sex. For many people, a sudden change in sexual frequency can increase anxiety, leading to self-doubt and catastrophic thinking: "It's been two months since the birth of our child, and she's still not interested in having sex with me. Even the nurse said it's okay to start having sex again. I always had a feeling that this would happen." Often, a simple awareness of the correlation between increased stress and low sexual arousal dampens the taking-things-so-personally reaction.

However, if you're the type of person that looks for validation in sex (i.e., thinking "If my partner desires me, than I'm a desirable person"), you may find yourself going down a spiral of self-doubt and blame. What happens next is often some combination of sulking, gossiping (about your partner), attacking, or cheating, all of which increases the possibility that no sex will be had anytime soon, or it will be the type of sex that is worth forgetting.

As I stated, it is helpful to know that sexual arousal and activity ebbs and flows in all healthy relationships. It is also important to be clear, with yourself, as well as your partner, about what you would like. If you're unable to have these conversations, it can be helpful to discuss your options with an impartial third person, such as a family or marriage therapist. Whatever you choose to do, your goal is to find ways to soothe your anxiety and over-reactivity. If you can do this, you may find yourself calmer and more in control of your emotions. As a result, your partner might "catch" what you've got, and respond in kind.

With dialed down reactivity and soothed hurt feelings, some closeness may come back into your relationship. With some patience and personal disclosure, sexual arousal may be right around the corner. The good news? You might find yourself having better, and more mature sex than you ever imagined.

4.2 Faulty assumptions about sex

It certainly seems logical that all the things we strive for in a monogamous relationship — comfort, security, love, familiarity — should lead to more enjoyable experiences in the bedroom. Yet if this book is teaching you anything, it should be to question your assumptions when it comes to relationships. So why doesn't it always work out that monogamy means better times in bed?

Comfort and security can actually sow the seeds of future sexual problems. Esther Perel, a marriage and sex therapist, suggests that although the beginning of a romantic relationship can be awkward, it also offers the excitement of danger, seduction, and novelty.

These elements are a key part of what makes new connections so passionate and satisfying. But as relationships develop, and we strive for friendship and security, troubles loom ahead. Therapist Esther Perel writes, "On some level we trade passion for security, that's trading one illusion for another. In desire, there must be some small amount of tension. Withered desire is all too often the unanticipated side effect of a growing intimacy, not one that's cooled." Seems like a cruel twist of fate.

All our efforts to establish healthy, mature relationships based on friendship, shared values, etc., can grow naturally into a situation of low sexual desire; all the more so once you introduce parenting to the mix. I'm not advocating for relationships where comfort, security, and emotional intimacy are nonexistent. However, I am suggesting that these attributes must be balanced by a sense of mystery and risk, particularly when it comes to sex. This means going beyond your comfort zone, and finding ways to grow past limitations and insecurities. And that's where things get interesting.

Just because you've decided it's time to experiment with a new sexual position, doesn't mean your partner is going to respond, "Fantastic, I've been waiting for you to ask me to do that!" There's a good chance your request will be met with anxiety and reluctance. If you require validation from your partner to feel good, you'll be hurt that he or she isn't particularly thrilled by your suggestion. This often causes a ping-pong effect, causing you to withdraw from each other, and even less sexual activity. That's why it's so important to understand the impact of anxiety and fear on sexuality, particularly in long-term relationships.

4.3 A focus on technique and tools

Because we assume that good sex is a natural byproduct of healthy relationships, we become distraught when things go wrong. Often, a quick-fix solution, like those on the magazine covers in my local grocery stores, seems like the answer, especially if we're worried that our relationship is broken and needs to be fixed right away. There's also an entire industry happy to sell you on the idea that all your relationship is missing are some Viagra and vibrators. In and of themselves, these tools can be helpful. However, they aren't a cure and are often used to avoid more pressing emotional issues. When used alongside self-improvement strategies, there's no question that sex toys, medication, and maybe even pornography can spice up a sexual relationship.

Before that happens, however, we have to be able to tell the difference between the cart and the horse. Because our sexuality reveals so much of who we are — physically, emotionally, and spiritually — it is fraught with meaning. When sex is grand, we use otherworldly terms to describe the experience: *She brought me to heaven*. However, when things go awry, blame and shame bounce rapidly back and forth, unveiling deep-seated fears and insecurities. Partners might ruminate about what or who is at fault, pondering, *Why doesn't she want me anymore? Am I unattractive to her? Is something wrong with her?*

When sexuality wanes, and couples turn to tools and techniques for help, they may be sidestepping the real issues. New positions and toys can stop a couple from confronting deeper issues in their relationship.

Our society's hyper-focus on technique and toys leaves sex feeling empty of meaning. Sex therapist Trina Read believes our "orgasm or bust" culture moves us further and further away from the intimacy we say we want with our partners. When we focus most of our intimate relationships on the physical rewards, we reduce intimacy to the purely physical level.

She points out that when sex becomes a purely physical act, there is very little to no fulfilment. Without fulfilment, she says, individuals in a relationship begin to emotionally starve, growing disillusioned and drawing away from their partners and deeper into themselves. Quick-fix solutions like those on the magazine covers are just a Band-Aid, masking more profound problems, and preventing lasting change. Tackling them head-on is difficult, but could lead to real growth and change, creating meaningful, lasting improvements in the couple's sex life.

5. Prolonging Your Own Pain

> *"I find the prospect of advising slightly illicit."*
>
> — Dr.Peter Kramer, *Should You Leave?*

We all know emotional problems cause suffering. If somebody asked you if you felt like prolonging your suffering, over a relationship or anything else, you'd probably say no.

And yet, in an effort to remove pain, both our own and for those we love, we often drag out interpersonal problems that could be addressed head on, often for years. Jane Fonda was right when she (or more likely her publicist) came up with the slogan, "No pain, no gain." This expression alludes to a fact of nature: It takes pain to mature, build muscle, etc. Many psychotherapists, clergy, and advice gurus misunderstand emotional pain, depression, anxiety, and other symptoms, and try to get rid of them as quickly as possible without understanding that we sometimes need pain to break through our inertia.

These "experts" love to capitalize on our anxiety, and offer quick fixes, promising everything from weight loss to blissful sex - all within 30 days, with a money back guarantee! So, we hand over our lives to an expert (be that a professional, a self-proclaimed authority, or a friend) and hope their advice can offer a quick fix. What we're looking for here is a clear-cut, obvious answer, such as "Yes, you really need to break up with your girlfriend," or, "If he loved you he would spend more time with you." In addition to giving them our trust, we also hand over responsibility for our problems, in return for a magical formula for success. But change won't work unless we shoulder some of the responsibility.

Like the flu, anxiety and fear are contagious, and they both create enough distress to drive us to seek out quick solutions in order to find immediate relief. Just like navigating the pharmacy shelves when you have the flu, you'll also find a confusing array of remedies for emotional suffering.

There's another parallel here: Many of the most ineffective (but well-meaning) solutions will come from family and friends.

Why? You probably asked them for advice, and because the people closest to you are the ones who are most strongly affected by your moods, they need you to feel better to make themselves feel better. Lewis Carroll wrote in *Alice in Wonderland*, "She generally gave herself very good advice, though she very seldom followed it."

In Alice's case, this makes perfect sense, because of the truth in the old maxim is that advice has more to do with the advice giver than the person seeking the advice. But because relationships are inherently difficult for so many people, asking for and receiving relationship advice is usually the blind leading the blind, well-meaning as the giver may be.

When two or more anxious people gather, nervous energy coalesces around them. Subconsciously, their goal is to find the quickest solution, so both of them can start to feel calmer. Usually, these friends and family members are too emotionally invested in the situation. Not only do they feel our pain, but it's also difficult to watch a loved one suffer. So they offer quick solutions they hope will reduce their suffering ("Leave him, he's no good for you.")

One of the most "curative" factors of almost all therapies is actually just the simple fact that the therapist/counselor doesn't have a stake in the outcome. Friends and family also tend to give you the advice they would give themselves, even though you're a different person, in what's probably a very different situation. This is particularly true if they're struggling in the same area. Maybe they can't deal with this in their own lives, but they're more than happy to prod family and friends to do what they can't. That's why a lot of the advice you'll hear from nonprofessionals falls into the get-out-while-you-still-can category.

The advice-giver's thinking probably goes something like this:

Joe is really struggling in his relationship. Struggling feels bad — I should know, my wife and I have been struggling for years. Relationships should make us feel good and happy. Therefore, I'll tell Joe to dump her and find another relationship where he feels happy and satisfied.

So the problem with advice-giving is two-fold: family and friends have too much emotional investment in your well-being, plus they are too biased by their own circumstances to provide the necessary objectivity about your situation.

Strangers and advice columnists don't know enough about the particulars of your situation, like your background and unique circumstances, to really provide meaningful guidance. Think of this as the Dr. Phil effect. In five minutes, Dr. Phil can tell anyone what's wrong them and what they should do about it. The problem is, he knows almost nothing about that person or the situation. The advice is by design generic: He would give anyone in a similar situation the same advice.

Yet we do often need the support of others to help us through hard times. This is why it's useful to have a therapist who really understands you and your situation. Instead of rushed, biased information, this can provide a calm atmosphere, where thinking about the problem and potential solutions is encouraged.

6. What Now?

I hope you haven't been scared off with this up close and personal look at the dark side of committed relationships. Remember, these issues all arise naturally, and if you learn to control your own reactions, they don't have to be dealbreakers.

So far, we've looked mainly at the theory of how and why we hit the quagmires that all couples find themselves in at some point. As we'll see, while it's impossible to avoid some of these things, we can be more strategic about what to do when they occur.

As you'll see in the next chapter, we can improve our capacity to choose our responses, and manage our awareness that these hard times are designed to help us grow up, to cultivate the love that we are capable of.

Before we move on, let's recap what was discussed so far:

- The goal of self-growth is to become more highly differentiated, getting clear on and then sticking to one's principles in the face of opposition.

- Our adult relationships are largely shaped by relationships from our family of origin.

- A feeling-oriented approach to dating and love can create unstable, disappointing relationships.

- The best way to create more stable, mature relationships is to stop focusing on other people — either by encouraging them to change, or blaming them for some misfortune — and spend more time understanding how you have contributed (positively and negatively) to each of your current relationships, so you can set goals for yourself based on your own values.

- Excessive compromise, particularly early on in a relationship, may help avoid problems in the short run, but can cause bigger problems in the long run.

- Over-asserting your independence may also stem from low differentiation and the inability to withstand opposing views or a partner's emotions. These two tendencies, to compromise excessively or to over-assert, are expressed in relationships as pursuing and distancing. But if you do find yourself in a pursuer-distancer dynamic, that doesn't necessarily mean you're mismatched; you may actually be very well-suited to each other.

With a greater awareness of how relationships work, at least from a family systems perspective, you can learn new strategies to deal with these issues in all of your relationships, current and future. Also, knowing a little theory will help you manage the tough times that happen in all intimate relationships. Instead of being taken by surprise, you may find yourself with more options, and clearer thinking, able to chart a successful course through stormy seas.

Still, theory alone doesn't lead to healthier relationships. We have to understand why these ideas work, but to become a proactive partner in your own happiness, it can't end with theory. The next chapter covers the vital work of growing and avoiding these pitfalls.

3

Growing

> *"Someday I'll fly*
>
> *Someday I'll soar*
>
> *Someday I'll be so damn much more"*
>
> — John Mayer, "Bigger Than My Body"

In the previous chapters, I shared pieces of my journey, to show you how relationships offer your best opportunity for self-growth. Now, we'll take a look at how relationship problems serve an essential function: They create the right amount of tension to kick-start change. Relationship problems can provide the energy that allows us to grow beyond our childhood wounds, and overcome inertia. Unfortunately, the inverse is also often true; when it comes to emotional growth, we either mature or regress; there is no standing still.

The key is, when you hit relationship snags, you've got to do something. Even Freud, the king of talk, understood this. I remember reading that he ended one of his therapeutic relationships by stating wryly (I'm paraphrasing), "OK, your analysis is now complete, now you have to go outside and buy some milk." His patient was incredulous; he pushed for more analysis. But Freud was adamant: Therapy was over, now he had to go and do something.

If you're in a relationship, I guarantee you'll encounter some or all of the problems we've talked about so far. So there are two critical questions you need to answer:

1. What do I do when my relationship runs into a problem?

2. How can I prepare myself before problems happen?

You must remember most of all to have faith in your own untapped potential. Beneath the veneer of your day-to-day coping mechanisms, complete with reactivity and defensiveness, you have the capacity to exhibit creative thinking, courage, resilience, and self-calm.

At this point, you may be thinking: Ha, that sounds lovely, but you don't know me or the crazy family I come from. Of course, you're right. But my experiences and my clients' have given me the optimism to believe that struggle and pain are surmountable, so long as they are leaned into rather than avoided.

If you're prone to lashing out emotionally, this section can help you find that part of you that is solid and focused. If you cave under peer pressure and are programmed to please others, it will help you find your ability to take a strong stand. And if you recoil from intimacy and physical closeness, it might start you on the path to enjoying the comfort, safety, and sensual experience of a warm physical relationship.

Where you stand today, emotionally, is ultimately a place of your own choosing. But that also means that at any given moment, you can decide to change the rules. You can become more reflective about your contribution to your own situation, and bring your best thinking and effort, with the goal of bettering yourself and your life.

1. Inertia versus Change

> "The forces that keep us doing the same thing have a higher degree of influence on us than the anxiety that change produces. So even though people talk about change, everything in the world they live in speaks to keeping it the same. And no matter how bad things are, at least it is familiar to us."
>
> — David Freeman

At the beginning of this book I shared a bit about my path from commitment-phobia to marriage. I did that to help explain how these ideas have helped many people like me and my clients. But there was another crucial time in my life when I was forced to choose between inertia and change. I hope it won't ruin the ending if I tell you right now that I chose change. The big question is how I managed to gain the courage and resolve to make it stick.

Like many people, I'm nostalgic about my childhood. When I was a kid, every season, every minute of every day, was an opportunity to embark on an adventure. A spiderweb or an abandoned house to explore provided an afternoon of fun and learning. My self-esteem was very much tied to my activities and hobbies. However, as I approached adolescence, I discovered that my quirky interests weren't winning me any popularity contests. In an attempt to avoid being a social outcast, and after a few not so pleasant experiences with bullying, I sought out more socially accepted ways to feel good about myself. For me, this revolved around collecting music and chasing girls. I stayed this way until my pre-midlife crisis, when I was 29 years old.

In my early twenties, I spent a brief but magnificent summer in Banff, Alberta, working as a chambermaid. (Yes, men do change sheets and clean toilets.) I returned home to Montreal, but remained fixated on the idea of returning west. Though I yearned to try, thoughts of revisiting this goal were fraught with anxiety. I didn't end up going back until my mid-thirties.

For example, whenever I entertained the notion of moving out west, I found myself simultaneously excited and at the same time, paralyzed with the fear of not being able to find work and a supportive community. Many of the factors that held me back, on some level, seemed reasonable, but overall, proved crippling. I wanted to please my parents and grandparents. I worried that I'd end up poor and lonely, far from home. This onslaught of worry built up into toxic anxiety. And instead of making the move, I found an outlet in promiscuity.

Some anxiety is healthy; without a little, it's hard to muster the energy and grit to take on life's challenges. Too much can quickly lead to paralysis.

I later found out I'd been dealing with what psychotherapist Robert Gerzon calls "natural anxiety," the realistic fears that encroach when contemplating growth. These aren't entirely irrational fears. Growth may indeed involve some risk.

However, having grown up in a risk-averse family that thwarted any attempts at change, I misinterpreted my natural anxiety as a red flag, indicating extreme danger. My mind swirled with worst-case scenarios: How will I find work? Why leave a job, an apartment, and the comforts of family and friends for uncertainty? What if the car breaks down on a stretch of highway without telephone service? Time and again, I'd retreat to the security and familiarity of the surroundings I knew but no longer wanted.

I rationalized that staying in my hometown of Montreal was the mature and healthy choice. I thought: I'd be nuts to do something that's making me feel uneasy. So I stayed. A few months later, out of the blue, I experienced my first panic attack.

My panic attacks provided a macabre gift, teaching me the painful lesson that playing it safe was not a recipe for serenity. I was experiencing what Robert Gerzon labels "toxic anxiety": being anxious about being anxious. It was only when the pain of inaction (staying in Montreal and continuing to experience worsening panic attacks) outweighed the anticipated pain of action (traveling by car across Canada) that real growth became possible.

I was forced to face either the anxiety of adventure and growth or the terror of wilting in a bland life. Now that the playing field was even, I chose adventure and the ensuing anxiety that would accompany this decision.

To my surprise, nothing horrible happened during my travels, and my panic attacks gradually went away. In fact, my decision to embrace action and adventure led to a whole cascade of good things. Life in Vancouver was rewarding and invigorating. Friendships made during that period of my life have remained some of my closest. My work was exciting and fulfilling; I founded and managed a music recording company for at-risk youth. I was creatively rejuvenated; I met a musical collaborator and we undertook a number of projects, including soundtracks for two feature documentaries.

Because so many aspects of our lives are intertwined, growth in one area has the capacity to impact many areas. As I increased my capacity to accept the unknown, and to take on risk and anxiety in my travels, I found myself bringing this courage and excitement into all areas of my life. Where before I had seen my fear of commitment as a character flaw, now it was something to walk towards, to overcome. Now, I could do something about it.

I want to be clear: This wasn't a miracle cure. Many of my initial attempts — whether in dating or trying to stay in a committed relationships — resulted in failure, or at least, setbacks. But where, in the past, I'd give up at that point and fall back on the excuse that I "just wasn't cut out for this sort of thing," now I had learned to walk towards fear. Taking on my fears and growing from them, I was finally able to explore emotional territory outside of my comfort zones. By staying with intimacy rather than running from it, I was teaching myself how to commit. Little by little, my level of differentiation was increasing.

It is an honorable act to walk towards the things you fear, and a process of self-growth to survive it. But there's no way of getting around this fact: Attempts to think, and act, with greater maturity, with yourself and others, will rarely be met with applause and kudos. Remember, systems resist change, and push for things to be the same. It is good to remember this bit of wisdom (paraphrased from the movie: *Three Kings*): "You do the thing you're scared of, and you get the courage after you do it."

There is a Jewish proverb that states: "He who can't endure the bad will not live to see the good."

2. Embracing Pain

> *"You make me want to be a better man."*
>
> — Melvin Udall (Jack Nicholson's character),
> *As Good As It Gets*

I've told you my story not because there's anything so special and wonderful about me, but the opposite. If I've achieved these results, others can, too. Once I began embracing, rather than fleeing from life's painful moments, I also began to discover how intimate relationships can help us grow. Rather than focus on a real story, I think a fictional one can best illustrate how this works.

Earlier in the book, we saw how the line, "You complete me," in the movie *Jerry Maguire* is a reminder of the common desire to find a partner who provides what we lack in ourselves, or the affirmation that we received as children in our family of origin. We saw that the intoxicating feelings experienced at the beginning of a relationship are a result of being completed, but that this very thing which drew us to our partner at first becomes an albatross around our neck later in the relationship. Efforts to recapture that early euphoria are futile.

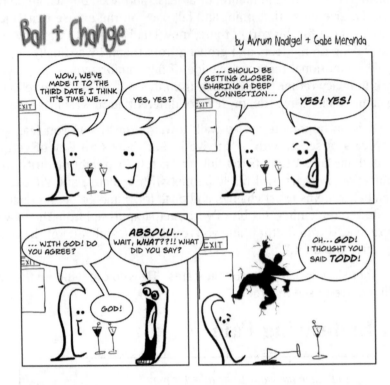

If *Jerry Maguire* captures the essence of how we pick our partners, I think James Brooks' *As Good As It Gets* points the way to how we can thrive together.

Without giving away too much of the plot (if you haven't seen it, it's a great movie) Melvin, played by Jack Nicholson, is a man wracked with anxiety and Obsessive-Compulsive Disorder. As the film progresses, we learn that much of his day-to-day activity is designed to keep his anxiety and obsessions in order. To say he has trouble with people is an understatement. Melvin's solid sources of comfort and meaning are caring for a dog, and his career as a writer.

As part of his OCD rituals, he frequents the same restaurant, and requests the same waitress and meals. This daily ritual allows him to develop an emotional attachment to his waitress, Carol, played by Helen Hunt. Carol serves him food, but also caters to his needs for dependability and cleanliness. Even before their relationship begins, Carol seems to "complete" Melvin, making him feel safe and cared for.

No wonder that, despite his attempts to remain secluded, Melvin finds himself drawn to Carol.

Later in the film, he's confronted with a frightening dilemma: stay the same and lose Carol, or deal with his crippling anxiety and embrace change. Here's the key: Just as I couldn't both stay in Montreal and move to Vancouver, Melvin can't have it both ways.

So, while out for dinner with Carol, Melvin takes a stand. Here's how it unfolds:

CAROL: Pay me a compliment, Melvin, I need one. Quick. And mean it!

MELVIN: Okay, I got a great compliment for you, and it's true.

CAROL: I'm so afraid you're about to say something awful.

MELVIN: Don't be pessimistic. It's not your style. Okay. Here I go. Clearly a mistake. I've got this … what? … ailment. My doctor, this shrink I used to go to all the time … he says in 50–60 percent of the cases, a pill really helps. Now, I hate pills. Very dangerous things, pills. I am using the word hate here with pills. Hate 'em. Anyway I never took them … then that night when you came over and said that you would never … well, you were there, you know what you said. And here's the compliment. That next morning, I took the pills.

CAROL: I'm not quite sure how that's a compliment for me.

MELVIN: You make me want to be a better man.

CAROL: That's maybe the best compliment of my life.

Melvin, and in turn, the audience, discover a deep truth about relationships and ourselves: Left to our own devices, we do not change. We say we want to change, but talk is often used as a tactic to avoid action. *As Good As It Gets* reminds us that our closest relationships can provide us with the exact amount of pain to spur growth.

Melvin understands that Carol is presenting him with an opportunity that he can't give to himself. If he takes the medication — which he dreads — he might be a better man. When he decides it's worth the risk, it's not because Carol told him to take the medication, but because Melvin finally gets clear on what he wants and this entails growing as a person. So he takes the medication, and moves outside of his comfort zone.

Unlike a lot of the messages coming at us in popular culture, there are many valuable lessons we can learn from this film.

2.1 Standing on our own two feet

Carol's ability to stand up for herself and muster enough self-respect to not be treated poorly by Melvin offers a lesson on creating healthy patterns in a relationship. She doesn't allow Melvin to blame his bad behavior on his psychological issues; she holds him accountable. This, in turn, allows Melvin to grow beyond his tired excuses and to search for a more mature way of being and interacting.

2.2 Learning to soothe our own anxieties

In the film, Melvin learns to rely on his own resources to soothe his fears and anxieties, resources he didn't even know he had at the start of the film; he learned these through his interactions. By relying on himself, he realizes that he doesn't need his partner for all the things he thought he did. That doesn't mean an offer of help or support from a loved one is inherently a problem. On the contrary, these acts can be gracious, warm, and loving. But when we expect and demand that our partners take care of us, we can become disillusioned when they are unable, or refuse, to fulfil our requests.

2.3 Taking risks leads to growth

Over the course of the film, Melvin and Carol both learn to deal with difficult issues that they face. They are able to do this thanks to the earlier risks they took with each other, and the personal growth that ensued. Focusing on self-improvement can heal relationships.

While in *Jerry Maguire* the focus was on what the other partner can do for you, here, Melvin focuses on improving himself. He does so without Carol asking him to, and with no guarantee that Carol will ever reciprocate his gesture.

2.4 Working on your relationship is a two-way street

You don't just work on your relationship, it also works on you. His relationship with Carol provides Melvin with a dilemma: Change or lose her. It thus forces him to work on himself.

Ball + Change

by Avrum Nodigel + Gabe Meranda

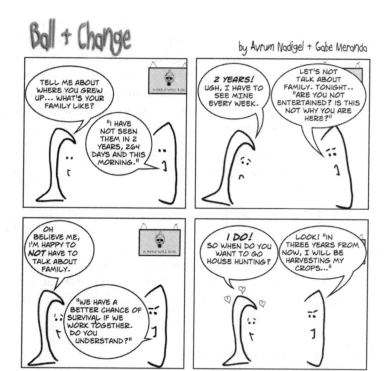

3. Preparing to Go Home and Work on Your Family of Origin

> "Be patient toward all that is unsolved in your heart and try to love the questions themselves ... "
>
> — Rainer Maria Rilke

So, we've spent a good deal of time exploring my life and the lives of other people I've met, both in my practice, in daily life, and those on the silver screen. Now it's time to turn the camera around for a minute and focus on you.

There are two types of people who purchase self-help or relationship books:

1. Those who want to change themselves.

2. Those who want to change someone else.

Attempting to change someone else rarely works. Unless someone asks you to help, people don't usually like to be psychoanalyzed (unless you're a professional), changed, prodded, or coached. Worse, they may actually be interested in changing, but your misguided efforts to speed things along might increase resistance and slow any growth. It can take a lot of restraint, but try to remember that it not only might not help, it could actually make things worse.

This section is for everybody else; those who fall into the change myself category. The following exercises and ideas are best approached with a sense of curiosity.

What do I mean by that? George Loewenstein, a professor of economics and psychology, wrote a paper titled "The Psychology of Curiosity." He explains that curiosity is a powerful state of mind that motivates us to move forward, discover new things, and fill in gaps in our knowledge. Conversely, a lack of curiosity fuels ignorance and rigidity, both in thinking and action. So, here are a few tools to cultivate curiosity about your own situation.

3.1 Broaden the picture

As you work through this book, try to look beyond the particulars of the individual stories to find patterns that may help explain the state of your relationships. For example, if you find that you constantly bicker with your mother about your choice of career, consider other factors in your family that would suggest anxiety around money and security.

Another approach would be to think about the function of the bickering; how does it serve your relationship? Perhaps it actually functions to keep you close. Often families prefer to continue experiencing conflict because they unconsciously fear they would become completely disconnected if they stopped arguing.

3.2 Cultivate good questions

Good questions stimulate thinking, and lead to more good questions. You might look at your family and figure you know them so well that you already have all the answers; you don't need to ask any more questions. You might say, "Look, I know why my parents divorced; my mother cheated and destroyed our family, end of story, nothing more to learn." For now, just consider that there might be more you can learn.

Challenge your own certainties with good questions. For example: Can my mother's affair help me understand their relationship better?

Was my father partly responsible for the state of their relationship? Were there other things going on that might have contributed to their marital strife (for example, a death or financial issues)?

3.3 Discover the story of you

Many of us grow up and don't give a moment's notice to the stories that preceded our birth. While our parents are alive, our need to know our family history lies dormant. Alas, it's usually after a parent or grandparent dies that we become hungry for family tales, in an attempt to better understand family members.

These stories also help you understand yourself better. The true richness of your life's tale extends way, way back before you were born. Making sense of your life without that information is like trying to figure out *Star Wars* after walking in midway through the movie (or watching *The Empire Strikes Back* before *Return of the Jedi*).

It's tragic when a yearning for more of our own history kicks in too late, after the best person to answer our questions is lost. Capture stories about the members of your family while you can. These are the tapestry of your life. They will help you in a million ways, filling in the details about why you act, think, and feel the way you do.

3.4 Be patient with yourself and others

Perhaps you picked up this book hoping it would help you get married by, oh, next week. Or, maybe you were hoping that some chronic issue would resolve itself if you could only find a magical ten-step process. If I could provide you with either of those things, I would. But two decades of this process have taught me that working properly on ourselves and on our relationships, however we choose to do it, takes time. I'm in the same boat: I am a work-in-progress, plugging away at being better in my relationships with my kids, my colleagues, and others. Like you, I have to remind myself to be patient.

The benefits of working through these strategies and improving your level of differentiation are immense. You have the opportunity to heal chronic issues that have plagued multiple generations of your family. And as you experience the benefits and start noticing improvements, you may want to reach out and involve other members of your family in the process, which could help them as much as you find it helps you.

Keep in mind, however, that attempting to change someone else rarely works. Other family members may or may not be as enthusiastic as you are. I hope you'll find some willing participants, ready to share stories and experiences from the past, but be prepared also for family members who are simply not willing to dredge up the past.

4. Studying Your Family of Origin

The biggest influence on our emotional lives is the families we came from. That's where we learned how to love, fight (fairly or otherwise), problem-solve, and a plethora of other behaviors, many of which we are not aware. While our family influences don't dictate exactly who we will date or how we'll fare in those relationships, they do supply us with most of the raw material that we have to work with in life.

That's why it can really help to study your family and get clarity on how the people and events helped shape who you are today. The following sections discuss some of the areas in which understanding your family can help most.

4.1 Offering perspective

Understanding your family members can remove the judgments and polarization that exist in all relationships. A little bit of history allows you to go from blame to compassion, or from, "My parents must have figured it was normal to yell at each other every night," to, "Oh, I didn't realize that my parents didn't start fighting until after my mother's cancer diagnosis. That explains a lot." This broader, more compassionate perspective can then be brought into your current relationships.

4.2 Objective assessment

Studying your family can help you understand objectively the rules and rituals that infuse the automatic behaviors in your particular family. This will provide the opportunity to choose what you'd like to keep and what you'd rather discard, according to how these behaviors align with your own values and principles. For example, if your family has a tendency towards confrontation, you can evaluate at what point your assertiveness turns into aggression and cut it off before it gets to that point, if you so choose.

4.3 Rethink your family dynamic

Doing this work may motivate you to choose different ways of interacting with certain family members. This could help you develop the ability to act, rather than react to the people in your life. As a result of making conscious choices, all of your relationships may see greater emotional health.

Ultimately, this work could improve your dating life and make you better prepared to enter into a commitment. That's precisely what it did for me. I believe that by understanding my family better, improving my relationship with them, becoming clearer on my values, and learning to deal better with my emotions and anxieties, I made myself ready to meet the right woman and settle down with her.

To better envision how this can play out in real life, we'll look at two people — one woman and one man — who are struggling with their dating lives. In the first example, Susan explores a relationship from her family of origin largely on her own. In the second, Greg does the same type of work while guided by a therapist. Hopefully, the two examples will give you an idea of which method could work better for you as you embark on the process.

4.3a Case study: Susan, on her own

Susan is a 25-year-old graduate student in psychology who has been dating Jeremy for approximately one year. While this is only her second serious relationship, she feels there is enough of a commitment to discuss moving in together. They get along great and rarely fight. When conflict does arise, Susan is quick to compromise to keep the peace.

Last month, Susan was devastated to learn that Jeremy was considering a job offer in Berlin. She was trying to be mature and reasonable, but she found herself angrily wondering why Jeremy would do this to her. However, she didn't say anything to him, trying hard not to make things worse.

Before long, Susan started to have trouble falling asleep, and could no longer concentrate in class; her grades began slipping. At home, she became unusually quiet and withdrawn. Jeremy asked what was the matter, but Susan rebuffed him. He took this personally and assumed he'd done something wrong. As tension increased, they started to bicker daily over small things.

Susan was saddened and perplexed by this. Her parents' relationship had been stormy, and as a teenager, she'd often escaped to her room to drown out their fighting with music. Susan had always blamed her mother, who was the only person raising her voice and constantly critical of Susan's father. Susan vowed to her closest friends that she was going to do everything differently. Yet here she was bickering with her boyfriend, deeply disconcerted to find herself in a similar situation to her parents'. Was history repeating itself?

During a family therapy course, Susan's professor introduced a tool known as a genogram, or family diagram. He discussed the benefits of creating a genogram to better understand the interdependence of family members. According to family therapist Dr. Ronald Richardson, this in-depth family diagram can help in a number of ways, as you can:

1. Discover and clarify exactly who your significant family influences are (not always the people who are the most closely related).

2. Fill in gaps of information about people and events that impacted you and other family members.

3. Help you begin interacting with family members in a more neutral, less reactive way.

The students were asked to create a three-generation family diagram — themselves, parents, and grandparents — and bring it back to class. They were to include names, ages, and significant dates and anniversaries (such as dates of birth, marriage, divorce, death). They were also instructed to select an event, a person, or a behavior they were curious about, and to write down a sentence about their understanding of how it came to be. Susan chose her relationship with Jeremy. She drafted a working hypothesis of what she thought was going on: Even though I act differently than my mother, Jeremy and I are fighting the way my parents did.

To start her family diagram, Susan used a software program to plot the basic details of her family. Genograms may look complex and daunting at first, but it doesn't take long to understand the basics.

Here's the genogram Susan created in Figure 1.

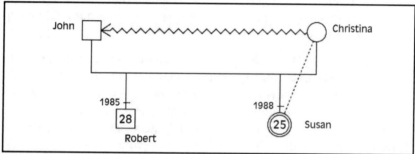

Figure 1: Susan's Genogram

In a genogram, males are indicated by a square, and females by a circle. Susan's father, John, is married to her mother, Christina, as shown by the solid line connecting the two. Her mother's frequent criticisms and bickering are shown by a squiggly line — representing conflict — with an arrow directed at her father.

Although Susan was often angry with her mother for mistreating her father, she was too intimidated to say anything. Throughout her adolescence, she avoided both parents. However, most of her energy went towards staying a safe distance away from mom, a pattern that continues to this day. This distance is indicated by the dotted line.

Next, Susan needed to speak to her parents to fill in the gaps from her diagram. Her instructor warned the students that family members might not take kindly to participating if they felt they were being blamed. He encouraged the students to gather facts about relationships and family members by emphasizing who, what, when, where, and how questions, but not why. "Why" questions can make people feel as if you're looking for a motive or a smoking gun. In other words, they might feel you are passing judgment on them. They then respond in a defensive manner, justifying their own behavior.

Keeping this in mind, Susan asked her mother how she had met her father. "What was your first date like? What qualities in him did you admire?" Later, she asked if her mother agreed with her observation that she and her husband had frequently bickered. She also asked her mother what she thought of her observation that they had a distant mother-daughter relationship.

At this point, Susan's mother started to cry. She knew that their relationship was somewhat estranged, but she hadn't been sure what to do about it. She told Susan that this was the last thing she wanted, and that it was especially painful because it was a repeat of her relationship with her own mother.

Susan asked, "When did you and Grandma become distant?" To her pleasant surprise, that question opened up the floodgates. "Oh, Grandma and I were never close," her mother responded, "She was always tiptoeing around your grandfather. When your grandfather would drink, into violence at times, she'd simply do whatever he wanted. It drove me nuts. I felt like she didn't protect me from his alcoholic rages. When I left home, I promised myself that I would never let myself be treated that way by any man. In a way, I chose your father because he was so kind, and quiet. I knew he'd never treat me the way my father treated my mother. And I knew I could stand up for myself, without any concern that your father would get violent."

By now, both mother and daughter were tearful. Susan told her mother, "Mom, I've never shared this with you, but I also promised myself that I'd be different from you. I thought if I was more agreeable, and less critical than you were, I could have a more loving relationship."

Her mother asked, "So are things different with Jeremy?"

"In some ways, yes, but in a lot of ways, no, which is a bit surprising."

"Well, sweetie," her mother said, "I guess there's some truth to the saying that the apple doesn't fall from the tree."

Later, Susan filled in the genogram with the information she gathered from her mother (see Figure 2).

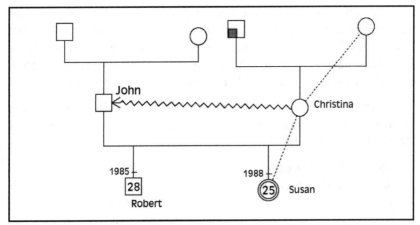

Figure 2: Susan's Revised Genogram

With only one interview, Susan had been able expand her understanding of her parents' struggles. She also felt like she had a better grasp on what she was up against with Jeremy. This wasn't a simply a matter of choosing the wrong mate, because her genogram seemed to indicate some sort of generational dynamic was being passed down the maternal line. While she wasn't yet sure what to do about it, she started to feel less reactive towards Jeremy.

As well, the interview softened some of Susan's resentment and blame. She still wished her parents had had a different relationship, but she blamed her mother less. It was hard to deny how similar Susan was to her mother. They both had an aversion to conflict, but chose different ways of dealing with it, just as Susan's mother had chosen a different response than her own mother had.

Back at school, Susan's professor encouraged her to continue the process with a person she wanted different experiences with but was currently not in conflict. *Well, that rules out Jeremy*, she thought. Based on the positive experience they shared while working on the genogram, she chose her mother.

The first thing Susan reflected on is how, ever since she was a child, she would wilt under the power of her mother's criticism. She also noticed that many of her discussions with her mother were about her father. While she enjoyed being her mother's confidante, she also felt it wasn't her place to receive this kind of private information. Ultimately, this too helped distance Susan from her father.

In an effort to improve the relationship, Susan planned to meet her mother, once a week in a neutral setting, for coffee. However, a few days before their first meeting, Susan started to feel anxious about spending so much one-on-one time with her mother. She cancelled the coffee date the night before she and her mother were scheduled to meet.

Frustrated, she returned to her professor and declared that she wasn't cut out for this exercise. "My mother is who she is," she said. "We've made it this far; why rock the boat?"

Her professor suggested that instead of going for weekly coffee — something they had never done and was thus too intimate for now — perhaps she could phone her mother once a week.

Susan reported back a couple of weeks later that they had made progress but that she would become emotional and reactive after six or seven minutes. "Great; keep the conversation to four minutes, then," her professor said "Set an alarm and politely end the call when it goes off. However — and this is critical — before you hang up, set up another time to speak in the near future."

A couple of days later, Susan called her mother and did her best to follow her professor's advice. She also took a risk and told her about some of her struggles with Jeremy. Her mother responded by giving authoritative advice about standing up to Jeremy.

Susan felt herself being triggered emotionally, so she stayed calm by using deep breathing exercises and reminding herself that the call would soon end. In a composed voice, Susan told her mother that she needed a listening ear, not a lecture. Her mother responded angrily and ended the call even before Susan's alarm went off. Susan felt the call was a failure. However, the next day she received a text message from her mother apologizing and asking if they could speak again.

Susan's professor congratulated her on her progress. He added that the goal was to stay true to herself for a bit longer every time, until she could sustain a coffee date and then a dinner. In turn, her mother would have to find different ways of being with Susan. As Susan developed more control over her emotional reactivity towards her mother, the more potential she would have to stay calm during times of high anxiety in all of her relationships. This would let her be more directed by her own beliefs and values rather than the feelings and opinions of others. For example, she would learn to temper her knee-jerk impulse to take care of other people's needs before her own.

For Susan to apply this growth to other relationships in her life in future, she will have to endure difficult conversations rather than avoid or flee them. It is a counterintuitive quirk of human nature that when we learn to tolerate the uneasiness of emotions and anxiety, conflict becomes less angst-ridden, not more. Riding out these harsh experiences over and over again will ultimately allow Susan to become more confident in her ability to stay calm and true to herself in the midst of these difficult situations.

Of course, the most important place she'll need these new skills is with Jeremy. She'll need to approach the situation not from a place of blame, but with a view to understanding the big picture, including her own contribution to the problem at hand. Unless she starts taking responsibility for her role in perpetuating the incessant bickering, she'll stay stuck on the idea that Jeremy's the one who has to change.

Without an honest assessment of her contribution, she'll never be able (or willing) to move beyond her default position of keeping the peace at all costs. In which case, she should probably expect the status quo to remain the same, or worsen.

However, if she's able to understand her part in this process she may be able to choose a different tactic for how she wants to act in this relationship. This opens up the possibility that she and Jeremy will find a new, healthier way of dealing with conflict.

Exploring your family of origin will undoubtedly open up emotion and anxiety. Some, like Susan, find that with minimal support — through some reading, research, and a few coaching or counseling sessions — they can manage the reactivity, in themselves or others, that emerges naturally when doing this work. However, many find it helpful to enlist the support of a therapist who will guide them through the process.

There are a few reasons you may decide to go this route. First, and most importantly, you might simply sense that it'll be too much to handle on your own. Or perhaps there is a lot of difficult family history that you know will be brought to the surface. This is especially true if your family has a history of trauma such as physical or sexual abuse, substance abuse, war, or displacement. In those cases, I strongly suggest seeking out a therapist to support you through this process. Even without significant trauma, a therapist can ease the process by helping you to reflect and remain calm.

A note about psychotherapy: There is a stereotype, propagated by filmmakers such as Woody Allen, that therapy requires weekly sessions for a decade or more, full of navel gazing but without substantial changes in the client's life. I'd like to assure you that there are more proactive approaches to therapy. The method I practice, family systems therapy, for example, is closer to life coaching, and aims for results far sooner than other approaches. Sessions begin once a week, but often move to bi-monthly and then monthly sessions. That's because we understand that growth does not happen in the therapist's office, but rather outside in the real world. There is an expectation that the client will do homework between sessions, and report back on progress (or lack thereof).

Let's now see how someone can go about this family exploration work with the support of a therapist.

4.3b Case study: Greg, with a professional

Greg, a 41-year-old executive director of a large nonprofit organization, contacted me because he was struggling with his fear of commitment. Recently, Tara, his girlfriend of nine months, ended their relationship because he was unwilling to discuss marriage or children. A few months had passed since then, but Greg couldn't stop thinking about Tara.

A few days earlier, Greg had bumped into Tara at the gym. They spent a few minutes chatting and Greg admitted that he still thought longingly about her. Tara then admitted that she was engaged to another man. Greg was stunned. In the past, Tara had always been willing to give him, and their relationship, another shot. Her great fear of being alone had before always allowed Greg to hold onto Tara without committing to anything too serious.

Greg was despondent. He reached out to a good friend for support. His friend suggested therapy.

"Look, Greg," said the friend, "I thought Tara and you were a good fit. I hope you don't take this the wrong way, but I'm thinking this has more to do with you than with the women you're dating. Why don't you spend some time single, and work on figuring out what's going wrong?"

In our first session together, Greg explained that he thoroughly enjoyed dating and courting women, but wanted me to know it was not just about promiscuous sex. The excitement of finding a woman and building a life together — in theory — excited him. However, as soon as things settled down, Greg would begin to feel claustrophobic. He said his chest would feel tight and he'd start to notice all sorts of imperfections in his partner. In the beginning, many of the women he dated would accommodate his requests to change things about themselves. But as each imperfection was fixed, he'd discover another one to take its place.

Frustrated, Greg told me he usually turned to friends for advice. Most told him if that he were with the right woman he wouldn't be feeling this way. Bearing this in mind, he'd fantasize about another relationship; one without imperfections and struggle. These thoughts excited him. And with that, Greg would soon be back in the dating scene, full of hope that this time will be different.

In our first session, I asked Greg basic information about his family. One key milestone was that Greg's parents divorced when he was eight years old. The years after that were full of arguments about finances and meetings with mediators and lawyers.

Greg tried to downplay the effect of the divorce: "I wasn't the only one; a lot of my friends were going through the same thing."

"I don't know about your friends," I responded, "but I do wonder what your parents told you about their divorce. How did they explain it to you?"

"To this day, they blame each other. My mom claims my dad may have had an affair, which he denies. My dad claims my mom never really loved him. I used to get really angry and sad about it. But now, it's just par for the course."

Greg and I created a three-generation genogram of his family. I believed that Greg's parents' divorce was key to understanding his commitment problems. That often happens with children of divorce, particularly of high-conflict divorces. Despite dismissing the possibility earlier, Greg soon came to the same conclusion, and decided to talk to his parents about their divorce and their views on relationships and love.

Greg met individually with his mother and father and asked them about their courtship, and about their own parents' marriages. Unfortunately, Greg reported back that both his parents had become too emotional and focused on blaming their ex-spouses to be of help. I suggested Greg approach his uncles and aunts to continue his research in a less emotionally charged realm. I made sure he kept in mind that everyone's perspective is subjective and should be taken with a grain of salt.

Greg was surprised to discover, through these interviews, that his parents were actually quite compatible when they first met. He also found out that his mother's father was dying of a prolonged illness that affected the entire family. In fact, he'd died just a few days before Greg's parents' wedding, leaving them planning a wedding and funeral the same week. Family members on both sides recalled this as a highly stressful time for everyone, especially Greg's parents.

I congratulated Greg for uncovering important information and encouraged him to keep peeling back the layers of his family story. Greg soon returned, having learned that, after his maternal grandfather passed away, there were numerous fights about wills and money. He remembers this from his own family, as his parents often fought about his mother's inheritance. Hearing this from outside family members let Greg place his parents' difficulties within the context of the stressors on the entire family. Greg slowly began moving away from blame to understanding, and eventually to compassion. He was still angry with his parents for their behavior, but began to realize that, as a young couple, they really had done their best to navigate a very stressful time.

With greater perspective came less anxiety and reactivity. Over time, Greg was able to speak to his parents more calmly, and talk to them about love and relationships. Greg discovered that his parents were as sensitive as he was about the issue of settling down. His mother was full of warnings about how to do things differently than she herself had done. She told him, "Something's missing in our family, some sort of marriage gene. Maybe it's best that we date, but not marry."

Greg's father was long on platitudes about love but short on how to handle day-to-day relationship difficulties. He believed in the romantic idea that love conquers all. When Greg asked why that hadn't helped his father's own marriage, he replied: "Because your mom doesn't buy into that idea."

Speaking to his parents didn't give Greg any shortcuts to help deal with his commitment anxiety, but it did make him feel less dysfunctional and alone, and with that, he found himself bolstered with a new-found energy to learn to do things differently.

A while later, Greg began dating again and made an important realization: Dating brought a refreshing vitality to his life. This also helped him realize why he became restless when the excitement of a new relationship was inevitably replaced by a comfortable intimacy.

We decided to explore his life outside of dating and relationships, to see what void he might be filling. What emerged was that Greg has a creative side that he had never fully explored. As a kid, he'd feel most alive when he was drawing and painting, but along with that came the crushing feeling of being told repeatedly by his mother that he wasn't particularly good at it.

In one of his ongoing conversations with his mother, which had started getting easier since he'd been consciously working on these issues, Greg found out that his mother had once been a sculptor, but gave it up over her own father's fury that she'd choose a career as an artist. Her father believed it was immature and selfish to risk her entire family's well-being with an unstable career. Breaking the pattern, Greg enrolled in a painting class. His goal wasn't to become a great painter, rather only to express this longtime passion.

As Greg began to feel better about himself, he also found that his life was more complete. Now that he had other sources of excitement, he found he'd become more discerning about the women he dated. No longer just filling a void, he consciously tried to meet a woman who would complement his life. Eventually, he met Rachel. Conversation was easy between them and they enjoyed similar activities.

After a year of dating, Greg and Rachel decided to move in together. Predictably, Greg felt his anxiety winding up again with renewed force. He started feeling critical of Rachel. However, unlike in the past, he dealt with his own feelings rather than expecting her to change to accommodate him. He came back to see me for a couple of extra booster sessions and, importantly, confided in his parents about his concerns. Surprisingly, both of his parents were able to empathize with his struggle to enter into a commitment. They even admitted their own regrets about not having been able to find a long-term, stable relationship.

Despite twinges of anxiety, Greg and Rachel's moving in together went fairly smoothly. Greg decided he no longer needed to see me regularly. He still comes in when his anxiety flares up over a big change in his relationship with Rachel, like their marriage and the birth of their first child. During these sessions, he also reports with pride on how he and his parents now regularly talk about his relationship, as well as their own relationships, past and present.

4.4 Family exploration: Getting started

Hopefully, the scenarios from the previous two sections — Greg's and Susan's stories — have demystified the type of family exploration work I'm suggesting you do, and demonstrated the great benefits of taking on this project, however difficult the going may be at first.

If you feel like you're ready to try, start with one relationship first, perhaps a close relationship you've long found difficult in some way. A good person to choose is a family member who triggers you emotionally. However, don't pick the person with whom you have the most conflicts either, as you might be biting off more than you can chew. Try to choose a relationship that you believe can survive the natural anxiety that often arises during this process.

Some of the questions you might ask yourself are: When did our relationship become troublesome? What external factors — financial stress, illness, moving far away — may have contributed to the current state of our relationship? Can I see my contribution to the fights we have?

To help expand your understanding of the relationship you're working on, start by drawing a genogram, as Susan and Greg did. Then, share your genogram with various members of your family. Ask them if the information is correct and to fill in any missing information. This is a non-threatening way to create curiosity and dialogue amongst your family.

Make sure to keep things objective, focusing on dates, places, and ages, rather than subjective, with its connotations of blame. This is what Susan's professor warned her about when he suggested she avoid "why" questions. For example, instead of asking your father if he regrets divorcing your mother, you might ask him if the dates of the divorce are correct. Or, who moved out of the house and when? More often than not, this more factual discussion will organically lead to a more substantial conversation.

When your family diagram is complete, tape it to a wall. Try to identify patterns and relationships that can flesh out the story of your family (and you). See if this story helps provide perspective on any of your current or past relationship or personal struggles. For example, you may notice that all firstborn males on your father's side function in a caretaking role. Given that you're a firstborn male, can you see this happening to you as well? What are the strengths and weaknesses of this position (based on what you've seen of the experiences of other firstborn males in your family)?

Next, use this information to create a hypothesis about the state of one or more relationships. For example, *I wonder if the bankruptcy of the family business led to my estrangement from my father?*

How do you know when you've found a worthwhile hypothesis? You'll know you're on the right track when your perspective is more nuanced, maybe even complex, rather than blaming one person for the state of a relationship. If you feel the time is right, you can speak further to your family and try to confirm or reconsider your hypothesis.

Often, this family exploration work leads to insight into your own functioning in the family. Perhaps you notice that you get anxious with your father, but not with your mother. Or that you have trouble being with your younger sister without giving advice and acting like a coach. Whatever observations you make, spend some time thinking if that's really how you want to relate to that person. Is there a better way? Are you operating from the best in yourself or from a reactive and imma- ture part? What can you change?

Here are some questions you might ask yourself, and areas for self-observation:

- Is this a new or old pattern?

- What am I feeling in my body when I talk to the family member in question? (For example, people often feel stress and anxiety as tightness in their shoulders or jaws.)

- What thoughts are going through my mind when I talk to this person?

- How do I usually respond to this reaction? Do I try to flee, leaving as quickly as possible? Do I become defensive or joke around to defuse anxious moments?

- How would I like to respond differently in the future?

Especially if you're working through these relationships alone, without a therapist, be careful not to bite off more than you can chew.

Sustained growth can only occur if you focus on one or two things at a time that you'd like to change. It's often best to tackle the easier things first. That way you build confidence in your ability to set a goal and achieve it. Later on, when you feel you're ready for a bigger challenge, then go for it!

Here are some warnings, largely drawn from the insights of family therapist Dr. Ronald Richardson in his book *Family Ties That Bind* (also published by Self-Counsel Press), on how to approach this work.

- Think about the countermoves other people will make, once you decide to change yourself or your relationships. How will you manage their reactions?

- If you focus on changing other people, you will most likely be defeated. Assume that there are powerful forces keeping people the way they are. However, change can be contagious, and if you're less anxious, more principled, and more goal-directed, others may choose to follow.

- That doesn't mean you should take a *quid pro quo* — I scratch your back, you scratch mine — approach. People can sniff out a scheme a mile away and will be resistant to change. So, while your change can cause a positive ripple effect, it's best not to count on it. Always keep the focus on yourself, and not on changing others.

5. Dating with Your Eyes Open

> *"If intense attractions could stop short of sexuality and revel in the delights of a 'separate, equal, and open' friendship for a protracted period, is it possible that those intense relationships would have more chance for long-term success?"*
>
> — Dr. Roberta Gilbert

STUART: She's incredible. I don't know what else to say.

AVRUM: Describe the perfection.

STUART: First of all, she's beautiful. I mean, when the door opened I thought, *I really don't deserve someone like this.*

AVRUM: What do you deserve?

STUART: I don't know, not her though. She's really funny. And seemed genuinely interested in everything I had to say.

AVRUM: Did you notice any differences between the two of you?

STUART: No, not at all. Isn't that a great sign?

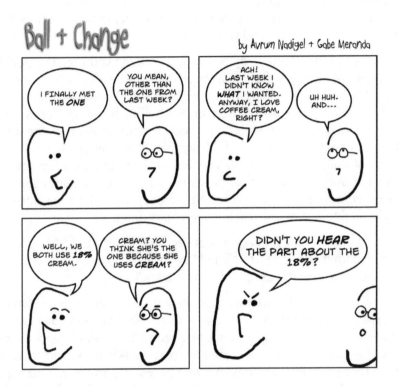

Stuart, the client in this example, is riding the exhilarating waves of infatuation and mutual admiration that so many of us enjoy when we date a new partner. And who can blame him? Besides illicit drugs, there is perhaps nothing as intoxicating as the throes of this early stage of love. The feelings are wonderful and we should enjoy them. However, if we lose ourselves entirely in those feelings, we stand a good chance of being blinded to the real person sitting across from us.

How can you date with your eyes open? And how can you be as honest as possible, letting potential partners see you clearly as well? As we've seen so many times already, blind love cannot last. Whether the shocking wake-up call happens a year or two down the road or early on in the relationship, the results can be ugly, sometimes tragic. Faults that could have been accepted slowly seem instead like fatal flaws. If the couple has already moved in together or taken their first steps on the road to marriage, they may now feel they've made a colossal mistake. Going in with eyes wide open can help avoid these disastrous situations.

Obviously, we need to take a clearheaded approach to dating, accepting the notion that it is better to truly know each other, warts and all, and then make the conscious decision to move forward together. Of course, that's easier said than done.

Let's face it: Dating is by nature a Darwinian venture. The goal is to weed out poor matches in order to find good matches. That means the odds of a date leading to a long-term relationship are extremely low. I'm talking the worst hitter in baseball history low. That's a lot of strikeouts. So it's no wonder so many become anxious at the mere thought of dating. Add to that the seemingly unlimited choices in the world of online dating, the exhaustion of repeating the same stories over and over, and the real or imagined judging eye of a stranger, and it's no wonder people use cosmetics, money, bravado, even outright lies in an attempt to hide their vulnerability and fear.

This sense of inadequacy is best captured in Groucho Marx's letter of resignation to the Friars' Club: "I don't want to belong to any club that would accept me as one of its members."

If we go with the premise that you can only control your own actions, then that means you should focus on how you approach dating. Leadership coach John Engels suggests good business hiring practises lend themselves well to choosing a life partner. When choosing a mate, try to take your time, and observe your potential partner interacting in a variety of situations. How is he with his own family of origin, and with meeting yours? What is it that draws him to you? (And what does that say about each of you?) What is she like under stress? When nobody is watching? Don't avoid the tough topics, as disagreements will give you the added benefit of noticing how he handles conflict. Behavior, past and present, is far more reliable than words when it comes to predicting how the future will be with someone.

Engels also encourages people to avoid choosing or rejecting partners based on one single criterion. For example, "She's really smart and has a great career. I think she'd make a good partner for me." Or, "He's wonderful in so many ways, but I can't stand the way he dresses. Makes me wonder if I could really be with him."

If you're prone to this type of single-criterion decision-making, Engels suggests that this may reflect a general reactive pattern of making decisions based on raw emotion rather than taking a step back and thinking clearly. In other words, the difference between going into decision-making blind, or with your eyes open.

Engels encourages people to evaluate potential dates based on a total package, one that might include the following criteria: physical attraction, sense of humor, financial goals, religious values, and family issues. The criteria you pick should stem from what's important to you and to the people with whom you share your life.

One way to figure out what themes you would like to focus on, in determining these criteria, is to consider your nonnegotiables. In other words, figure out the most important parts of your life, then decide what they need to look like for you to be happy and fulfilled. A good place to start would be your own family of origin. What ideas or traditions worked for you? What would you like to pass on to your own family? What would sadden you if it weren't passed on? What things would you like to improve upon or get rid of altogether?

Alternatively, during any given day, pay close attention to what grabs your attention. What are you curious about? What gets you excited? What political or social issues do you stand for? These can be important clues to figuring out what values are important to you, what inspires you, and what enriches your life.

I'll give you an example from my own life. As I wrote at the beginning, I went into the early part of my dating life with my eyes closed. As I entered my early thirties, I made a concerted effort to try dating with my eyes open wide. As a result, I began dating women who resembled more closely the type of person with whom I could imagine building a life. But I still wasn't prepared for the question my future wife, Aliza, asked me during our first phone conversation.

Our exchange was filled with laughter; we were both clearly excited by our mutual interests and the connection we seemed to have. Partway through the conversation, however, she grew more serious and said, "I need to ask you two questions, Avrum: Do you want to get married? Do you want children?"

Until that point, I had always assumed these types of topics were off limits until a few weeks into the dating process. I figured an ambivalence about serious topics, such as parenting or future goals, might be misunderstood, leading to someone walking away from what might have developed into a good relationship.

Alas, Aliza asked the question, forcing me to confront myself. I could hear from the tone of her voice that if I mumbled some wishy-washy answer the conversation would be over. I paused, looked into myself, and said, "Yes. Yes, I want marriage and children."

That question had a few consequences. First, my respect for Aliza developed right away. It took guts for her to ask; this showed me that she was a woman ready to stand up for her convictions. Second, it started off our relationship with the important questions already on the table. Our eyes were open rather than closed.

Earlier in this chapter, I wrote that you can only control your own actions and reactions and thus your approach to dating. That doesn't mean your approach can't have an effect on the people you attract and the way they approach dating. Look at Aliza's question to me about having children. Her thoughtful approach to dating increased my ability to ask her, and myself, the difficult questions, and to make sure we were moving forward towards the mutual goals she'd boldly put on the table. So while you can only control your own thoughts, feelings, and actions, you can certainly affect another person and the dynamic that exists between you.

Are all your friends and family telling you the opposite? You will certainly never see this sort of sober approach to dating in a Hollywood movie (it would probably make a really dull movie). But dating isn't the same as a job interview, so you can't approach it the same way.

While the above may sound a bit methodical, and lacking the whiz-bang of popular dating blogs — it is the type of sober thinking that will help you pick better partners. But this does not preclude bringing some creativity, fun and risk-taking into the date planning equation. If you're the type that doesn't like to date, perhaps it's because you're getting too caught up in what a date is supposed to look like. Or, what you have to act, dress, and/or talk like. Forget all that — bring your best self into your dates. So if you're the type that enjoys rock climbing, and not going for drinks, suggest that for a first date. If your date scoffs at the idea outright, you may have saved yourself some time and money. Or, if you collect vintage comic books, see if you can squeeze that interest into one of your dates. Hey, it worked for Clarence Worley, the character played by Christian Slater in the movie *True Romance*. The better able you are to represent the best in you — values, goals, interests, hobbies, etc. — the quicker you'll discover if the person you're dating is worthy of another date, or life commitment.

4

Moving Forward

> *"We've won it. It's going to get better now. You can sort of tell these things."*
>
> — Robert M. Pirsig,
> *Zen and the Art of Motorcycle Maintenance*

For many of you, this book is just the beginning of your journey. I hope you are starting to see relationships and the challenges they bring in a different light from what the media, family, and friends are telling you.

These new perspectives may just give you a chance to begin feeling and acting differently. If you transform the way you interact with your loved ones, there is a good chance they too will begin to change. This isn't a guarantee, but I've seen it happen many times.

Before you embark on your journey to commitment, I'd like to share two pivotal moments that proved to me that I was indeed growing, at a time when I wasn't yet convinced. I knew I was thinking differently and maturing, but other, more immature parts of me were not ready to let go. Change increases anxiety, and if you aren't prepared for this you risk losing your way. But even with preparation, anxiety can have its way with you. It is a cruel joke that, just when we think we've licked a personal struggle, things can suddenly take a sharp turn for the worse. For me, this took the shape of two dreams.

The first dream occurred when I was one year into my relationship with Aliza:

> *I'm standing next to my red Honda Civic, Aliza by my side.*
> *We start to hug, and I notice my left arm is slowly fading*
> *away. Then my right arm starts to go, and next it's my chest.*
> *My girlfriend is oblivious to the fact that she is hugging air.*

I remember waking up in a total panic, thinking, Clearly, this is a sign from my unconscious that I'm in the wrong relationship!

Thankfully, I know a thing or two about dreams, especially that we must approach dreams as metaphor, rather than fact. They certainly shouldn't be used as a basis for making major life decisions.

I made a few notes about the images in my dream and my feelings towards them, and then shared the notes with my therapist. Together, we explored this disturbing dream. Partway through the session, I began to understand that the dream was both a warning and a kick in the pants: You don't really know who you are or what you stand for. You are at risk of losing yourself, of disappearing, as you accommodate the needs, desires, and wishes of your partner.

In other words, I'd end up like my parents; in an unhappy relationship, blaming my spouse for my lot in life, with no idea how to use my struggle to help me grow.

That was the warning, the motivational shove to be like Ebenezer Scrooge, and use my dream to mature. To do so, I would need to stay true to my values and principles, while remaining with my partner. I did not have to disappear; there were other options.

A few days after proposing to Aliza, I had a second dream:

> *I'm standing on a small rickety bridge, the ones you find*
> *in small towns (and horror movies). There is only enough*
> *room for one car to cross at a time. On the other side of the*
> *bridge is my fiancée. I cautiously make my way across the*
> *bridge. Suddenly, the wooden planks break apart and spill*
> *into open space, crashing into the water below. I drop to*
> *my knees, paralyzed with fear. Unable to move, I watch the*
> *bridge continue to give way. There's no way to go back to*
> *my side of the bridge. Since I'm petrified of falling, I begin*
> *to crawl across the bridge, being careful to avoid the gaps*
> *and jagged wooden edges. Though I'm getting closer to the*

other side, I feel there is no way I'm going to be able to work
around the chasms, and with that thought, the dream ends.

Again, I brought the dream to my therapist. In that session, I came to appreciate that the dream represented progress in the face of my fears. In reality, I was no longer disappearing in the face of intimacy, though in my dream my safety and comfort were crumbling all around me. Yet I still crawled to the other side of the bridge. I didn't careen off into the water below or run back to my side of the bridge, which represented safety and comfort. My dream had showed me what I knew somewhat in my conscious mind: To move beyond my fear of intimacy and marry Aliza, I would need to let go of the emotional scaffolding that kept me safe, albeit alone and single. There would be no other way.

The Chassidic sage Rabbi Nachman of Breslov was fond of saying, "The entire world is a narrow bridge, but the important thing is to not be afraid." I'm not sure how one crosses these bridges without being afraid, but cross you must, if you wish to make the most of your relationships and your life.

So embrace your struggles. Get clarity on your default patterns and reactivity. Try to recall times when you functioned in the best possible way, calm, principled, creative, loving, and generous. If those times are rare, then capture what you can in a journal.

Remind yourself that it is possible to think differently and, in turn, act differently. In time you will actually be different, perhaps in ways that your parents, grandparents, and great-grandparents could never have imagined.

1. Next Steps

A few years ago, my wife and I were invited to a lunch, along with over a dozen people I didn't know. Some were paired off as couples, the rest were single. All of them looked to be in their twenties and thirties.

The host introduced me, and mentioned that I was writing a book about relationships. One of the women turned to me and asked what it was about. I mentioned my working title: "The best time to work on your marriage is when you're single". She said, "I agree, and often wonder if my fiancé and I should explore pre-marital counselling". Her fiancé, sitting next to her, replied: "I can't understand why anyone would do that. I mean, we don't have any major problems. Why start looking for things that could cause problems a few months before our wedding?" His fiancée sat there, stone-faced. Silence descended on the room. Worried I might be responsible for some rash decision this couple might make when they got home, I tried to redirect attention to another topic. So I asked someone to pass the egg salad.

By the way, jittery grooms aren't the only ones skittish about having these types of discussions. I recall an incident where I was promoting a workshop to a rabbi who works with young couples. He was concerned the material might sour what would otherwise be the most exciting time in a young person's life. He worried that many young people are already anxious about getting married, so why add fuel to the fire? Like the young groom above, the rabbi seemed to prefer a "don't rock the boat" philosophy.

Leaving lunch that afternoon, I was disappointed in myself. This had been the perfect opportunity to share my thoughts, with just the right audience for all the material I'd been putting together about committment and differentiation. For me, the moment was lost, but the lesson was not. With all the benefit of hindsight, I'd like to share the answer that I should have given that nervous groom then:

"Why mess with a good a thing? Good question. Would you say that, for a relatively healthy individual, exercise is a waste of time? Is it best to start weight training and cardiovascular exercise after you've discovered a weaknesses in your body? Most people, even those who swear they're allergic to sweat and gyms, know that preventive medicine - getting the right balance of exercise, sleep or nutrition - is the best way to prevent big problems in the future. They also know that any change in diet or exercise will be uncomfortable, to start with. In some cases, it will even be painful.

With a bit of knowledge and self-awareness, one can even use the discomfort to discover weaknesses you were not aware of - providing a roadmap where your diet and exercise regime could be directed.

Just as there's never a bad time to start exercising, it's absolutely true that you can work on your marriage anytime. But even a cursory understanding of physiology is enough to know that there are better times than others. Starting to work out when you are strong, well-rested and healthy will usually give you greater gains faster. Similarly, the best time to work on your marriage is when you're single: before the kids, mortgage... the full catastrophe of living. As Benjamin Franklin said, though I doubt he was on his way to the gym, "'An ounce of prevention is worth a pound of cure." A pound being years of psychotherapy, which for many couples translates to too little, too late.

If he was still listening, I'd be curious to find out more about that terrified fiancé's reaction. I'd love to ask him what he thought might happen, the worst-case scenario, if they did some premarital work on their relationship. I'd be curious to know, "If you were to agree to open things up just a little, which one or two niggling things in your relationship would you tackle?

Since you've read this far, I'm assuming you're less skeptical of the process outlined in this book.

Still, I might surprise the groom by telling him that a bit of skepticism - particularly in self-growth initiatives - can be good thing. By balancing strong feeling-states with some thinking, you can dig up some good questions and self-experiments. It is also very helpful to have a roadmap of what you're trying to accomplish. What are you trying to learn - about yourself, your family and your relationships? If you do try this work, how will you know your time was well spent, or wasted?

I ask similar questions to these when I meet a new client for the first time. This helps me get a better understanding of what they're hoping to accomplish in therapy. Asking these questions also lets me to clarify any misconceptions about what I can and can't offer, and what they should expect from this journey.

When I've done my job right, the client leaves that first session with an expanded view of the problem. We accomplish this with many of the tools you've seen in this book: building a family diagram, a historical timeline, self-soothing techniques, self-experiments and a discussion of theory so they can understand the natural ways they and the people they love function in relationships.

Learning to commit is a lifelong venture. I've found that it's most helpful to start with a practical question, or a problem that is on your mind. That question could be about intimate relationships, but it doesn't have to be. Maybe you're asking yourself, "Why do I always seem to end up with these terrible partners, where it's immediately obvious to everyone but me that things aren't going to work out?" Maybe you're about to remarry; you want to do things differently this time around, but you still have some niggling doubts. Parts of your relationship feel terribly familiar.

Perhaps you're single, using an online dating site, and flummoxed that your profile is attracting the wrong people. It's easy to find fault with the medium and say, "Oh, online dating sites never work," or to feel it's the others' faults and think, "Why do I only attract creeps?." But maybe your profile needs to better reflect who you are, and what you stand for. This will require some risk taking on your part, in the form self-disclosure, honesty and courage.

Start with any issue or relationship that sparks the most curiosity, or trouble, when you think about it honestly. Next, it's time to expand the problem, or rather, the context in which you're viewing it. Place your central problem or question within the events of your life. When did it start? Has it been an issue since you were born? Since your grandfather died? Who is impacted by this? Only you? Your siblings? Is this something you're comfortable discussing this with your parents? If so, have they found themselves in a similar situation ("Oh, you know us Greenbergs, we're all a little nutty during tax season.")? Are there parallels within their marriage that you may have witnessed growing up?

As you gather this data, it can be helpful to plot it on a timeline, or genogram or family diagram. In my practice, I do both. Two seemingly unrelated events take on new meaning when you see them objectively on a whiteboard. Even if your issue seems to have no bearing on the family you grew up in, it still can be useful to make a rough sketch of your family. Start with the facts such as names, births, deaths, illnesses, etc. Plot the major players on the diagram. If you're feeling a little more ambitious, perhaps add relationship data, like who's not speaking to who, or who is the family outcast, etc.

Now, step back. What do you see? Perhaps a bigger picture is beginning to emerge.

If you feel comfortable sharing what you've discovered, ask a sibling, parent, friend or partner to take a look and comment. Does your problem look different when you see it on a timeline ("Hmm, I didn't realize my dad lost his job three months before my anxiety started to act up.")?

On your timeline, jot down the most important events of the past five years, or for the five years before the particular problem you're exploring began. How many events took place over those five years? How did those events impact the players in your family and your life? How did they impact you?

Now, I suggest you sleep on it. There's no need to rush to find an answer for any of these questions. The goal is to get a better understanding how people, and you, function in your family. With this information, you will be better able to think about changes you'd like to make in your life.

After you've had some time to think about this, do you have any new thoughts, or new ways of understanding your question or dilemma?

Perhaps this work will help you identify some unfinished family business passed down from the previous generation. Now that it's landed in your lap, you may be inspired to take on some new projects in your own life.

Personal projects usually start with a question or a curiosity: "I wonder what would happen if I told my dad that I'm going to pay my own rent? Could I survive? How would he react? What would I need to do to nurture my own financial maturity? Would this make me more able to discuss my financial goals and concerns with someone I'm dating?"

Sharing what you've discovered about your own history can be another type of personal project. Is there someone you want to try to engage with, to talk about past events with a bit more curiosity, and a greater distance than you've been able to talk about them before? Share your family diagram and timeline with this person. Does he or she agree with some of your observations?

Although this type of project is meaningful, don't get too caught up in the other person's reactions. Even if the other person decides not to participate, you have gained the prize of understanding these important dynamics better, and by extension, how you function in relationships as well.

This is where Bowen's concept of differentiation, discussed earlier, can be most valuable: helping you better understand your own struggles with intimacy and commitment.

In my own life, this has been tremendously helpful, and it's central to the work I do with my clients. It's essential to understand that not differentiating, not becoming your own person, can be the most comfortable choice. However, with those, come the predictable problems of stunted growth. On the other hand, to love fully, to live with creativity, equanimity and peace of mind, requires you to take the leap and become an autonomous person.

It sure isn't easy, but the results are so worth it: being clear about your own values and principles and living by these truths. I have seen firsthand — personally and professionally — what becoming an authentic adult looks like. The process isn't always pretty; it can be fraught with turbulence and "tsk, tsks" from those closest to you, but the payoff is immense.

1.1 Tips going forward

Work on your relationships by tackling relationships within your family of origin and learn to increase your differentiation as you go. Date with your eyes wide open and don't write people off over one minor criterion. You can work through your pain and fear of intimacy if you make a conscious choice to change. Here are a few tips for moving forward on your journey:

- Choose one relationship on which to actively work.

- Be patient with the process.

- Let go of any expectation that people will, or should, accompany you on this journey (though often they will).

- Whenever you find yourself thinking you have someone figured out, think again. Few people ever fully understand themselves, let alone those closest to them.

- Track your efforts and the lessons learned. Journaling is an excellent way to do this. Danny Gregory's *The Creative License* is an enjoyable, excellent tool for self-exploration.

- Nourish your dreams and goals, through money, time, and attention.

- If you find yourself getting overwhelmed, or stuck, remember what a big task this is that you've taken on; don't be afraid to seek help from a relationship coach or therapist who can help you with the process.

What I wish for all of us, myself included, is the patience and fortitude to allow our relationships to do their work, turning us into the people we're destined to be. This is truly the best gift we can give ourselves, our partners, and our children.

Resources
for Further
Reading

Bowen, Murray. *Family Therapy in Clinical Practice*. Maryland: Jason Aronson, 1978.

Covey,Stephen. *The 7 Habits of Highly Effective People: Powerful Lessons in Personal Change*. New York: RosettaBooks, 2013.

Freeman, David. *Multigenerational Family Therapy*. New York: Routledge (1991).

Gilbert, Roberta M. *Extraordinary Relationships: A New Way of Thinking About Human Interactions*. New York: Wiley, 1992.

Gregory, Danny. *The Creative License: Giving Yourself Permission to Be the Artist You Truly Are*. Hyperion, 2005.

Kramer, Peter. *Should You Leave?: A Psychiatrist Explores Intimacy and Autonomy — and the Nature of Advice*. New York: Penguin Books, 1999.

Lerner, Harriet. *The Dance of Intimacy: A Woman's Guide to Courageous Acts of Change in Key Relationships*. New York: Harper Perennial, 1997.

McGoldrick , Monica. *Genograms*. New York: W.W. Norton & Company, 2008.

Richardson, Ronald W. *Family Ties That Bind: A Self-Help Guide to Change through Family of Origin Therapy*. Vancouver, BC: Self-Counsel Press, 1984.

"The Crucible 4 Points of Balance," Dr. David Schnarch for the Crucible Institute, accessed March 16, 2015, http://crucible4points.com/crucible-four-points-balance.

Schnarch, David. *Passionate Marriage: Keeping Love and Intimacy Alive in Committed Relationships*. New York: W.W. Norton & Company, 2009.